A Reminder of What Democracy Is

Clarity, Courage, Everyday Action

for a Stronger Future

GAIL WEBSTER

Copyright Page

Copyright © 2025 by Gail Webster

All rights reserved. No part of this book may be reproduced or transmitted in any form or by any means, electronic or mechanical, including photocopying, recording, or by any information storage and retrieval system, without prior written permission from the publisher, except in the case of brief quotations embodied in critical articles or reviews. Copyright case #1-15009821541

ISBN (Paperback): [pending or number]
ISBN (Hardcover): [pending or number]
ISBN (eBook): [pending or number]

Library of Congress Control Number: [pending or number]

Publisher: HW Premier Publishing LLC
Spokane, Wa
www.hwpremierpublishing.com

Cover design by Gail Webster
Interior design by Gail Webster

Contents

Introduction 7
    What You Can Expect From This Book 8
    Why This Matters Now 9

Chapter 1: Democracy in Fog: Why Confusion Weakens Civic Life 11
    The Democracy "Fog" 13
    What Fuels the Fog 14
    Reflection: Where Do You Feel the Fog? 15
    The Civics Gap and How We Close It 16
    Doomscrolling and Distrust: How News Overload Paralyzes Us .. 17
    "Isn't Voting Enough?" Why Many Feel Helpless or Disengaged .. 19

Chapter 2: Demystifying Democracy: Foundations for Everyone 22
    Beyond Ballots: What Actually Makes a Country Democratic? 23
    Reflection: The Team Sport Test 24
    Rule of Law, Free Press, Fair Elections: A No-Jargon Guide 25
    Republic vs. Democracy: Clearing Up the Confusion 26
    Democracy in Daily Life: Power Dynamics in Classrooms, Chats, and Workspaces 27
    Inclusion, Not Perfection: How Marginalized Voices Strengthen Democracy 28
    The Global "Democracy Playbook": Lessons from Five Continents 30
    Receipts Matter: How to Fact-Check Claims About Democracy ... 32

Chapter 3: Threats in the Now: Spotting the Real Problems (and What's Just Noise) 34

    Modern Authoritarians: How Elected Leaders Undermine Democracy 35

    Social Media Algorithms and the "Echo Chamber" Trap 37

    Disinformation 101: How Falsehoods Spread 38

    Warning Signs: How Democracies Slip Toward Authoritarianism . 40

    "Us vs. Them" The Hidden Costs to Community 41

    "Us" is good. "Them" is bad. 42

    Holding the Line Together 43

Chapter 4: Digital Literacy: Tools for the Democratic Age 46

    Spotting Disinformation Red Flag 46

    Disinformation 201: Building Immunity to Lies 48

    Prebunking & Cognitive Resistance 48

    Deepfakes & Synthetic Media 49

    Breaking the Echo Chamber: Why It Feels So Good (and So Dangerous) 50

    The Algorithm's Trap 50

    Why It Matters for Democracy 51

    Comfort vs. Truth 52

    Tools for Everyday Digital Defense 53

Chapter 5: Real People, Real Change : Stories and Lessons from Everyday Democracy 56

    Immigrant Voices: Expanding the Democratic Conversation 57

    Youth at the Forefront of Democracy: The Power of Student Movements 59

Women on the Frontlines of Democracy 60

Faith Communities and Democracy 63

Local Heroes: Everyday People Defending Democracy 64

Bridging Divides: Dialogue Across Differences 65

Democracy at the Dinner Table 67

Heroes of Everyday Democracy 68

Chapter 6: Everyday Actions: Your Personal Democracy Toolkit 71

Your Civic Action Plan: Personalizing Participation for Your Life 71

Micro-Actions with Macro Impact: Democracy in Five Minutes a Day 73

Volunteering Beyond Elections: Year-Round Opportunities for Change 74

Grassroots Organizing: Building from the Ground Up 75

Digital Town Halls: Hosting and Participating Online with Impact 76

Public Comment That Gets Results: Emails, Calls, and 60-Second Testimony 77

Chapter 7: Building Resilience: Community Strength in a Polarized World 80

Resilience Starts Local: Why Strong Communities Matter 81

Strength in Numbers: Collective Action When It Matters Most 82

Everyday Habits That Make Communities Stronger 84

Facing Hard Truths Together 86

Civic Education as a Shield 87

The Power of Collective Hope 89

Chapter 8: Democracy for All: Centering Diversity and Global Perspectives 91

    Innovation at the Edges: Technology as a Democratic Tool 91

    Global Lessons in Diversity and Inclusion 93

    Learning From Setbacks: How Movements Rebuild 95

    The Road Ahead 96

Chapter 9: Choosing Hope: Renewal, Resilience, and the Future We Build Together 98

    Resilience in Crisis: How Democracies Bounce Back (and How You Can Help) 99

    Cultivating Hope: Why Optimism Is a Civic Responsibility 101

    Building Your Crisis Action Plan 102

    Measuring Your Impact: Tracking Progress in Everyday Democracy 104

    Building Digital Democracy: Tools for the Next Generation 105

    Beyond the Bubble: Digital Platforms for Democracy 107

    Your Democracy Journey: The Challenge to Take Action Today. 108

Conclusion 111

Acknowledgements .... Error! Bookmark not defined.

References.. 115

Leave Review... 120

Appendix: Tools, Checklists, and Prompts 121

    Appendix A: Democracy Job Requirements Checklist 121

    Appendix B: Responsibilities of a Democratic Voter..................... 121

    Appendix C: Civic Action Tools.. 122

Appendix D: Reflection Prompts 123
Appendix E: 30-Day Civic Sprint Playbook 125
Appendix F: Vigilance in Action 130
Appendix G: Digital Defense Checklist 132
Reflection: Practicing Digital Defense 133

Introduction

"The dogmas of the quiet past are inadequate to the stormy present. The occasion is piled high with difficulty, and we must rise with the occasion." — Abraham Lincoln, 1862

Figure 1: Lincoln Memorial (Public Domain)

Democracy is often described in lofty terms: freedom, equality, the will of the people. But in daily life, it rarely feels so simple. Instead, it feels noisy, overwhelming, and sometimes discouraging. We scroll past headlines warning of a 'democracy in crisis.' We argue with friends or family, then wonder if it was even worth bringing up. We wonder whether our voices matter.

That fog of confusion is real. And it has consequences. We tune out. We stop trusting. Eventually, cynicism sets in. But it doesn't have to be that way.

This book is about finding clarity not by pretending democracy is easy, but by facing its complexity honestly and practically. You'll see how everyday people, in small and sometimes surprising ways, push back against cynicism and keep democracy alive. This isn't just theory; it's full of tools you can use right now, in real life, to cut through the noise, rebuild trust, and take action beyond the ballot box.

This book isn't about being perfect. It's about showing up confused, curious, hopeful and finding your way through the noise.

What You Can Expect From This Book

Let's be honest: books about democracy often disappoint. Too many read like soapbox speeches — one-sided, scolding, convinced the author alone has the truth. You pick them up hoping for clarity and walk away feeling boxed in.

This book will not do that.

At its best, democracy is disagreement: messy, loud, imperfect, and inclusive. It creates space for all voices, even those we dislike or don't understand. Parties and elections matter, but they're not the entire story.

Here's what I'm committed to: listening more than lecturing, including voices from many sides, and offering hope that's grounded in real action. When I make a claim, I'll show you where it comes from, with concise notes at the end of each chapter so you can check the sources yourself.

And the stories won't just come from pundits or politicians. You will hear from young organizers. They led walkouts. You will also hear from immigrants pushing for access in languages other than English, small-town leaders, and citizens in other countries. These citizens have seen their democracies falter and then fight to restore them. These voices aren't extras; they are the heartbeat of this book.

Each chapter will end with something practical you can do. No vague "raise awareness" talk. Just tools you can use.

That approach matters because the way we talk about democracy shapes whether people lean in or tune out. If the only voices people hear are polarized, preachy, or abstract, the fog only thickens. This book aims to cut through that.

Why This Matters Now

Democracy only works when people do. It doesn't run on autopilot, and it doesn't improve on its own; it responds to us.

Some people insist America is a republic, not a democracy. But those terms aren't opposites. A republic is simply one form of democracy, where we elect representatives to act on our behalf. What matters isn't the label, but whether people feel their voices truly count.

That might sound heavy, but here's the truth: democracy is not a relic to preserve under glass. It's a practice to carry forward. And that's why I've written this book for you.

If you've ever closed a book about democracy feeling smaller than when you started, I hope this one feels different: clear, respectful, and realistic.
Not false optimism but practical hope, the kind that grows stronger with each small step you take.

You won't find lectures or lofty theories here. Just stories, strategies, and small steps that add up because democracy doesn't require perfection.

It just needs people who show up.

Chapter 1: Democracy in Fog: Why Confusion Weakens Civic Life

"A people who mean to be their own governors must arm themselves with the power which knowledge gives." — James Madison

Figure 2: James Madison (Public Domain)

Picture a thick fog rolling over a city. Landmarks you once relied on vanish into the haze. The streets you walk every day now feel uncertain. That's what democracy can feel like today.

Before the fog, things feel solid: you know where the courthouse is, you believe your vote is counted, and you trust the rules apply fairly. In the fog, those same landmarks blur. Headlines contradict each other, a neighbor's post online sparks suspicion, and even basic questions — *What's true? What's fair?* Seems impossible to answer.

This fog is thickest online, where news and opinions collide in real time. Scroll your feed, and you'll see half a dozen versions of the same story. One post screams that democracy is under attack. Others shrug it off as exaggeration. Still others hint at conspiracy. Even if you try to dig deeper, there's always another layer — viral videos with misleading captions, infographics that twist statistics, comment threads where facts get buried under arguments. Social media gives everyone a voice, but it also amplifies rumors and half-truths at lightning speed. Instead of clarity, we get an endless storm of conflicting claims, each one seeming urgent and true.

The consequences are real. I've met young adults who once voted with optimism but now skip elections entirely. *"It's too much,"* one tells me. *"I don't know what's worth paying attention to anymore."* That's not apathy; it's self-preservation in a confusing world.

I've also spoken with older voters who, after decades of broken promises and endless scandals, quietly walked away. *"I used to believe my vote mattered,"* one man admitted. *"Now it just feels like shouting into the wind."* His words carried the weight of disappointment, a slow erosion of trust built up over years.

And the cost goes beyond missed votes or silent news feeds. When people cannot make sense of the world, cynicism takes root: *All politicians are corrupt. Nothing ever changes. My voice does not matter.* These aren't throwaway lines. They are warning signs. When enough people stop believing their voices count, we all lose the power to shape our shared future. The fog wins not because people stopped caring, but because they stopped seeing a way forward.

Reflection: Where Do You Feel the Fog?
Pause here. Think about your own experience. Jot down three recent moments when you felt overwhelmed or frustrated trying to make sense of democracy.

- **Maybe it was an argument with a friend.**

- **Maybe it was a confusing headline.**
- **Maybe it was a story online you weren't sure was true.**

Don't judge yourself or try to "fix" it. Just capture the moments. Those moments matter because they prove the confusion isn't just in the headlines; it's in our everyday lives. And that's why this chapter begins here: the fog isn't permanent. And none of us have to navigate it alone.

The Democracy "Fog"

Imagine a thick fog rolling over a city. Landmarks you once relied on vanish into the haze. The streets you walk every day now feel uncertain. That's what democracy can feel like today.

Before the fog, things feel solid: you know where the courthouse is, you believe your vote is counted, and you trust the rules apply fairly. In the fog, those same landmarks blur. Headlines contradict each other, a neighbor's post online sparks suspicion, and even basic questions — *What's true? What's fair?* — seem impossible to answer.

This fog is thickest online, where news and opinions collide in real time. Scroll your feed, and you'll see half a dozen versions of the same story. One post screams that democracy is under attack. Other shrug it off as exaggeration. Still others hint at a conspiracy. Even if you try to dig deeper, there's always another layer — viral videos with misleading captions, infographics that twist statistics, comment threads where facts get buried under arguments. Social media gives everyone a voice, but it also amplifies rumors and half-truths at lightning speed. Instead of clarity, we get an endless storm of conflicting claims, each one seeming urgent and true.

I've also spoken with older voters who, after decades of broken promises and endless scandals, quietly walked away. *"I used to believe my vote mattered,"* one man admitted. *"Now it just feels like shouting into the wind."* His words carried the weight of disappointment, a slow erosion of trust built up over years.

And the cost goes beyond missed votes or silent news feeds. When people cannot make sense of the world, cynicism takes root: *all politicians are corrupt... nothing ever changes... my voice doesn't matter.* These aren't throwaway lines. They are warning signs. When enough people stop believing their voices count, we all lose the power to shape our shared future. The fog wins not because people stopped caring, but because they stopped seeing a way forward.

What Fuels the Fog

Several forces fuel this confusion, and each one has grown stronger.

Decades ago, most families tuned into the same evening broadcast. Walter Cronkite and Peter Jennings told everyone the same story at the same time.
Today, your uncle gets his news from Facebook, your sister scrolls TikTok, and you skim whatever headline pops up first on your phone. The shared starting point is gone.

Algorithms sharpen the divide. They don't just deliver news — they decide what rises to the top. Outrage, sensational headlines, and emotional triggers spread fast. A neighbor might click on one heated post about election fraud, and suddenly their feed fills with more of the same. Even well-meaning friends, thinking they're "just sharing what they saw," end up spreading half-truths or outright fabrications.

Our current crises include the pandemic, climate disasters, economic uncertainty, and political polarization. These issues have reshaped daily life, become more frequent, and made the future harder to envision. They also turn neighbors into opponents. Confusion isn't the exception — it's the new normal.

And nobody is immune. I've watched seasoned journalists pause mid-broadcast to fact-check themselves in real time. I've heard teachers admit they don't know what sources to trust anymore. Even politicians, the very people we expect to project certainty, often look bewildered by the speed of change. If you've ever felt lost or unsure, you're not alone; you're in the company of experts who are still trying to catch up.

But here's what I've learned: recognizing the fog is the first step to navigating through it. When we name it for what it is not ignorance, not apathy, but an overload of change and noise we can begin, together, to find a way forward.

Reflection: What Fuels *Your* Fog?
Take a moment to notice which of these forces feels closest to your own life:
- Do you feel overwhelmed by the flood of online news and posts?
- Have you seen a friend or family member share something you knew wasn't true?
- Has a big crisis like the pandemic or economic uncertainty left you questioning what comes next?

Write down one or two examples. You don't need to solve them; just acknowledge them. Noticing the source of the fog is the first step toward finding clarity.

Reflection: Where Do You Feel the Fog?

Pause here. Think about your own experience. Jot down three recent moments when you felt overwhelmed or frustrated trying to make sense of democracy.
- Maybe it was an argument with a friend.
- Maybe it was a confusing headline.
- Maybe it was a story online you weren't sure was true.

Don't judge yourself or try to "fix" it. Just capture the moments. Those moments matter because they prove the confusion isn't just in the headlines; it's in our everyday lives. And that's why this book exists. The fog isn't permanent. And none of us have to navigate it alone.

The Civics Gap and How We Close It

Have you ever wished you knew more about how the government functions? If so, you've already identified a key issue: the difference between what we learn in school and what we need as citizens. Civics class is supposed to be the place where it all clicks. Teachers hang up flowcharts of the three branches of government. You memorize the legislative, executive, judicial branches. The test comes, you cram the night before, and then let it all fade beneath algebra, sports, part-time jobs, and everything else life throws your way.

For many, that's where the story ends. Years later, you're at a dinner table. Someone brings up "rule of law" or "checks and balances." A quiet panic creeps in. You nod, hoping nobody asks you to explain. That discomfort isn't laziness or ignorance — it's the residue of an education that stopped at memorization. Most civics classes teach democracy like a machine you can diagram but never drive.

But real life is messier. Separation of powers sounds straightforward until you watch branches of government push and pull through court battles, executive orders, and bitter headlines. That's when the questions come: *"Isn't someone supposed to stop this?"* or *"Why does it look so chaotic?"* Democracy's messiness extends far beyond Washington, D.C. You can see it in school board disputes, statehouse debates, or local councils where neighbors clash over zoning, budgets, and policy.

And the challenge isn't just remembering terms; it's keeping up in a world that changes faster than textbooks can. Imagine being a teacher in 2024, standing in front of students while their phone's buzz with breaking news about political scandals or global protests. Old lesson plans feel obsolete against that backdrop. Even teachers struggle sometimes in admitting they don't know which sources to trust.

It wasn't until I saw democracy working differently elsewhere that the pieces clicked for me. In Taiwan, everyday citizens use digital platforms to debate policy, propose laws, and hold leaders accountable. Suddenly, "public participation" wasn't just a term from civics class — it was alive, immediate, real. It showed what democracy looks like when the fog clears: ordinary people not just memorizing systems, but shaping them in real time.

Have you ever been afraid to ask basic questions, or wondered if democracy is just a school subject? Let me tell you: as an adult citizen, your questions matter more than any test you took as a teenager. School may have left you with half-finished answers, but the story of democracy is still being written, and your voice is part of the next chapter.

Doomscrolling and Distrust: How News Overload Paralyzes Us

Late at night, phone in hand, thumb flicking endlessly through TikTok, X, or Instagram, you've probably done it. We all have. There's a word for it: doomscrolling.

You scroll looking for clarity, but what you find is a torrent of bad news: one headline bleaker than the last, one video more urgent, one thread more hostile. You promise yourself just one more post. But instead of feeling informed, you feel drained, like your energy leaked out through the screen.

This isn't just a bad habit. It's a psychological trap. A constant stream of crises, election disputes, violent protests, and endless scandals doesn't just keep us updated — it overwhelms us. It blurs the line between urgent and background noise. Every headline feels like a five-alarm fire. You might wake up to five alerts about democracy "in crisis" across the globe before you've even had breakfast.

Here's the subtle danger: doomscrolling erodes trust. Not only in politicians or institutions, but in the news itself — and even in your own instincts.

When everything shouts BREAKING!, EXCLUSIVE!, MUST READ!, it's hard to know what's worth your attention. You start second-guessing: *Is this important? Am I being spun?*

Even careful people slip. Maybe you've shared a post with a misleading caption or repeated a rumor that sounded just believable enough. When you realize it was false, it stings. And it plants a seed of doubt about your own judgment.

This personal experience isn't just anecdotal. Studies confirm what many of us feel: doomscrolling doesn't motivate; it discourages. After enough time scrolling, people pull back. They stop talking about issues with friends. Some even skip voting. The constant negativity shrinks our sense of agency. Apathy isn't always laziness; it's a defense mechanism.

And worse, trust itself frays — not just in media or government, but in facts themselves. When trust collapses, polarization deepens.

Dialogue shuts down. When enough people retreat from civic life, democracy loses the engaged citizens it needs to function. Doomscrolling doesn't just paralyze individuals; it poisons the shared information environment we all depend on.
But there's a way forward. Later in this book, I'll share tools for digital literacy: how to separate fact from fiction, set healthier limits on news, and build a "media diet" that informs without overwhelming. You don't need to ignore reality; you just need strategies to keep it from swallowing you whole.

You deserve information that helps you act, not news that leaves you paralyzed. The difference matters — not just for you, but for all of us.

"Isn't Voting Enough?" Why Many Feel Helpless or Disengaged

Growing up, we're taught that Election Day is when democracy really happens. Casting a ballot is presented as the golden ticket to being a "good citizen" the moment your voice finally matters.

So when I voted for the first time, I was proud. That little "I Voted" sticker on my jacket felt like a badge of honor. I walked out believing I had made a real difference, that I was part of something important.

Then the results came in. Win or lose, nothing in my life changed. Bills still stacked up. The same problems filled the news. My vote felt like a drop in an endless storm.

I'm not alone. Friends, classmates, coworkers — they all have their own versions of this story. They show up to vote, but when nothing changes, disappointment sets in. Some stop showing up altogether. Others keep voting but privately wonder if it matters. If democracy is only about one day every few years, no wonder so many people think: *Maybe my voice doesn't matter after all.*

This isn't just frustrating; it's draining. It frames democracy as something that sleeps between elections instead of something alive in daily life. When one bubble on one ballot doesn't spark change, cynicism creeps in. People tune out. And when enough people tune out, democracy loses the daily participation that actually makes it work.

But here's the truth: democracy doesn't live in a single ballot. It breathes in the space between elections. It lives in everyday actions — neighbors organizing food drives, students pushing for safer schools, friends correcting misinformation in group chats. It's in city council questions, school board meetings, and local volunteer projects.

None of these make national headlines, but they ripple outward, shaping communities, shifting culture, and slowly changing the bigger picture.

Genuine change rarely comes from one vote. It comes from a thousand small actions multiplied by millions of people. That doesn't mean voting isn't essential; it is. Casting a ballot is one of the clearest ways to be heard. But it's not the only way. When we treat it as the whole story, we shrink democracy to a single moment. When we see it as one part of a larger, ongoing practice, we strengthen it.

Democracy doesn't happen just once every few years; it happens every day, and it needs you to show up for more than just elections.

In the chapters ahead, we'll explore how trust is built (and broken), why information matters more than ever, and how small daily choices ripple outward into collective power. Because democracy's story isn't written by institutions alone — it's written by us.

Chapter 2: Demystifying Democracy: Foundations for Everyone

The price of democracy is the ongoing pursuit of its ideals, not the assumption that they're already secure."– Unknown

Democracy gets talked about a lot, but ask ten people what it really means, and you'll hear ten different answers. Some point to elections, others talk about rights, and a few might shrug, admitting they're not sure anymore. That confusion isn't a sign of failure; it's a reminder that democracy is layered and alive, not just a word in a textbook.

Figure 3: Opening page of the U.S. Constitution 1787
(Public Domain)

Too often, we treat democracy like a scoreboard. Did we vote? Did we elect someone? End of story. But what happens between elections matters just as much, if not more. The real test is whether the game is being played fairly: Are the rules applied equally? Are referees honest?

Do all players have time to take part, or are some pushed to the sidelines?

This chapter demystifies democracy, revealing it as a system based on principles relevant to everyone, from students to voters. We'll look at what really makes a country democratic, why those foundations matter, and how they show up in daily life.

Let's step onto the field together, not just watching the score, but paying attention to how the game is played.

Beyond Ballots: What Actually Makes a Country Democratic?

Imagine walking into a buzzing stadium on game day. The scoreboard is flashing, but you're not just watching the numbers. You're watching the action on the field. Are the players following the rules? Are the referees fair? Is every teammate having time to play, or are some pushed aside for no good reason?

Democracy works the same way. Too often, people point to the scoreboard — elections — and say, *"Look, we voted, so we must be a democracy."* But that's only the surface. Elections matter, yes, but real democracy is about what happens before, during, and after the vote.

Think of democracy as a team sport. Everyone has to play by the rules, not just celebrate when their side wins. Courts, legislatures, leaders who obey the law, and a press free to question those in power — these are the pillars holding up the stadium. When one of them weakens, the entire game tilts. You can still hold elections, but they risk becoming rigged matches where the outcome is set before the first whistle blows.

Separation of powers is like having trustworthy referees. If one branch of government grabs too much control, the others are there to step in and call foul. This keeps any single player from rewriting the rules to benefit their own interests.

And democracy isn't just about majority rule. Protecting minority rights is just as essential. Imagine a team voting never to pass the ball to one player because of her shoes. Even if the vote was "fair," that isn't real teamwork. True democracy ensures every voice matters, even when outnumbered. Constitutions and courts exist for that very reason — to shield people from being trampled by the majority.

Some countries settle for surface-level democracy. They hold regular elections but clamp down on the press, jail opponents, or ignore court rulings. Leaders allow people to vote, but silence journalists or quietly change the rules. It might look like democracy on paper, but in practice it's hollow.
A free press, independent judges, engaged citizens, and accountable officials are all essential for democracy. Without these, you're left with a shell of democracy that collapses under pressure. With them, people can trust the game again not because it's perfect, but because it's fair enough to keep playing.

Reflection: The Team Sport Test

Think about a group you are part of, maybe a class project, a sports team, or your job. Who makes the rules? Who gets heard? What happens when someone breaks an agreement? Who steps in as the referee? Look closely and you might notice where deep democracy is alive in your circle and where it is missing.

Rule of Law, Free Press, Fair Elections: A No-Jargon Guide

"Rule of law" may sound like something only lawyers worry about, but it affects daily life in real ways. At its core, it means nobody is above the rules — not presidents, not prime ministers, not even mayors or school principals. Imagine a school where teachers can break rules whenever they want but punish students for the same thing. That wouldn't feel fair. In a real democracy, if leaders lie under oath, abuse their power, or break the law, there must be consequences. Court cases, investigations, and sometimes even removal from office are proof that the rule of law is alive. When rules apply equally, trust grows. When they don't, democracy wobbles.

The free press is another pillar that keeps democracy standing. Journalists are watchdogs. They ask hard questions, uncover hidden truths, and share news with the public—whether leaders like it. Imagine a reporter exposing corruption at city hall and publishing the story without being fired or threatened. That is the free press at work. Viral videos of misconduct, leaked documents, or investigative reports are all modern examples of how the press strengthens democracy. But when authorities silence or jail reporters simply doing their jobs, the warning lights are flashing.

Fair elections also go beyond simply letting people cast ballots. "Free" elections mean you can vote without fear of violence, bribery, or intimidation. Elections that are "fair" mean officials count each vote honestly and give it equal weight. When someone stuffs ballots, jails opponents, or redraws voting districts to favor a specific side, the elections turn into a performance rather than a choice.

These principles aren't abstract—they shape how people live and how much trust they place in their system. If you doubt the fairness of elections, or you believe courts are biased, caring about outcomes becomes harder. That doubt spreads and weakens the entire system.

Free and fair must always go together. One without the other leaves space for abuse. Every time you see journalists expose corruption or courts push back against illegal power grabs, you are witnessing these democratic pillars at work. And every time they weaken, even strong democracies wobble.

Republic vs. Democracy: Clearing Up the Confusion

If you've ever wondered whether the U.S. is a "democracy" or a "republic," you're not alone. Politicians, teachers, and even neighbors toss these words around—sometimes as if they mean totally different things. The truth is, America is both.

At its core, democracy means government by the people. Citizens hold the ultimate power, either directly or through their votes. But a republic is a specific type of democracy. A republic relies on elected representatives. These representatives are bound by a constitution. The constitution safeguards individual rights and protects the minority.

Think of it like this: democracy is the principle that power belongs to the people. A republic is the structure, the system of elected leaders, checks and balances, and constitutional guardrails that keep that principle fair and balanced.

This distinction matters today. Sometimes, when people say, "We're not a democracy, we're a republic," it's used to downplay the value of broad participation. But that misreads history. The Founders created a republic because they believed democracy needed structure and protections to thrive. Elections alone aren't enough; rights must be safeguarded, power must be limited, and institutions must be able to hold leaders accountable.

Understanding this clears up one of the biggest myths — that democracy is "mob rule." A healthy republic ensures that majority decisions can't trample fundamental rights. Both the words democracy and republic accurately describe America, and together, they explain why your vote, your voice, and your rights matter.

Reflection Prompt: When you hear leaders or commentators use the words "republic" or "democracy," what do you think they're really emphasizing? Write an example from recent headlines, maybe about voting rights, court rulings, or presidential elections, where the distinction came into play.

Democracy in Daily Life: Power Dynamics in Classrooms, Chats, and Workspaces

Democracy doesn't live only in parliaments or on TV when politicians argue. It also shows up in the everyday places you spend your time in classrooms, group chats, and offices. These small circles are where democratic habits are learned and practiced.

Take a student council election. At first glance, it might look like nothing more than a popularity contest. But when debates happen and promises are kept, it becomes a practice run for real democracy. Students hold leaders accountable, expect answers, and push for fairness. That mirrors the values of a functioning democratic system.

Group chats reveal similar power dynamics. Sometimes one person makes every decision about what movie to watch, where to hang out, and others go quiet because it's easier than speaking up. This is how some voices disappear. But when the group takes a moment to invite, everyone's input or votes on a plan, the result feels fairer, and people stay engaged.

Workplaces are another window. In some jobs, decisions are handed down with no explanation, leaving people powerless and frustrated. In others, leaders explain their reasoning, ask for suggestions, or even let teams vote on small choices. Transparency builds trust. People feel their voices matter, not just their labor.

These patterns show up everywhere, and you don't need formal authority to change them. Implement democratic values in your groups immediately. Encourage quieter members to speak, suggest voting when needed, and rotate leadership. Consensus works when people take the time to talk through disagreements. Quick voting works when decisions need to move forward. The point is to make space for everyone.

Paying attention to who holds power, who gets overlooked, and how decisions are made is training for larger systems. Practicing democracy in daily life prepares us to expect it and demand it in the bigger arenas where it matters most.

Inclusion, Not Perfection: How Marginalized Voices Strengthen Democracy

Democracy doesn't live only in parliaments or on TV when politicians argue. It also shows up in the everyday places you spend your time in classrooms, group chats, and offices. These small circles are where democratic habits are learned and practiced.

Take a student council election. At first glance, it might look like nothing more than a popularity contest. But when debates happen and promises are kept, it becomes a practice run for real democracy.

Students hold leaders accountable, expect answers, and push for fairness. That mirrors the values of a functioning democratic system.

Group chats reveal similar power dynamics. Sometimes one person makes every decision what movie to watch, where to hang out and others go quiet because it's easier than speaking up. This is how some voices disappear. But when the group takes a moment to invite, everyone's input or votes on a plan, the result feels fairer and people stay engaged.

Workplaces are another window. In some jobs, decisions are handed down with no explanation, leaving people powerless and frustrated. In others, leaders explain their reasoning, ask for suggestions, or even let teams vote on small choices. Transparency builds trust. People feel their voices matter, not just their labor.

These patterns are not new. For most of history, many voices were excluded from decision-making women, people of color, immigrants, people with disabilities. That exclusion didn't just silence individuals; it limited the perspectives and solutions available to leaders. The result was weaker decisions that ignored the needs of entire communities.

When those voices pushed their way in, democracy grew stronger. The women's suffrage movement expanded political representation and brought new attention to maternal health and family policy. The labor movement pushed for workplace safety that protected everyone. The disability rights movement secured accessibility improvements — curb cuts, ramps, captioning that ended up helping parents with strollers, workers moving heavy loads, and older adults too. These gains didn't come easily. Each movement wrestled with internal debates and strategies, but the result was undeniable: inclusion expanded freedom for all.

The process continues today. In one school district, immigrant parents pushed for translation services at board meetings. At first, it seemed like small accommodation. But the change meant families could fully take part in decisions about their children's education, and the entire school system benefited from broader engagement.

These patterns show up everywhere, and you don't need formal authority to change them. You can promote democratic values now. Invite quieter people to speak, suggest votes, or rotate leadership. Consensus works when people take the time to talk through disagreements. Quick voting works when decisions need to move forward. The point is to make space for everyone.

Paying attention to who holds power, who gets overlooked, and how decisions are made is training for larger systems. Practicing democracy in daily life prepares us to expect it and demand it in the bigger arenas where it matters most. When people say democracy is alive, they don't mean it's perfect. They mean democracy works as intended — being challenged, questioned, and improved.

The Global "Democracy Playbook": Lessons from Five Continents

The challenges we've discussed aren't unique to any one country. Around the world, different societies have found creative and imperfect ways to strengthen democratic participation. These examples don't offer blueprints, but they do show possibilities worth learning from.

In Taiwan, experiments with digital platforms like *vTaiwan* and *Pol.is* have created new forms of consultation. Citizens share feedback on issues ranging from Uber regulations to same-sex marriage, and the government uses these discussions to inform decisions. The legislature still makes the final call, but the process shows how technology can broaden participation beyond traditional town halls.

In South Africa, the Truth and Reconciliation Commission offered a forum for testimony after the end of apartheid. It created a space for truth-telling that helped some communities move forward, even as its long-term impact remains debated. Inequalities persist, prosecutions were limited, and reconciliation is unfinished — but the attempt itself showed how confronting the past can be part of democratic rebuilding.

In Ghana, repeated peaceful transfers of power since the 1990s have built trust in electoral outcomes. That trust wasn't automatic; it came from transparency efforts that included international observers, civil society monitoring, and active citizen insistence on fair rules. Ghana's experience shows that when institutions and citizens reinforce each other, elections can become a source of confidence rather than conflict.

In Finland, schools treat media literacy as a civic skill. Students learn to identify misinformation and practice spotting bias as part of their curriculum. This investment isn't glamorous, but it equips citizens to navigate an information landscape where facts and falsehoods mix freely.

Taken together, these stories show that democracy adapts through inclusion, accountability, and education. None of these approaches are perfect or permanent. Each faces its own tensions, and each reflects the culture and history of its society. But they remind us that democracy is never static. It grows stronger when people whether in Taipei, Johannesburg, Accra, or Helsinki push for systems that listen, include, and respond.

Receipts Matter: How to Fact-Check Claims About Democracy

The global examples show that democracy adapts when people push for inclusion, accountability, and education. But none of that works if citizens can't tell truth from falsehood. In today's world, information itself has become part of the battlefield for democracy.

Memes can shape opinions faster than textbooks. A viral video can sway more people than a public debate. That speed makes fact-checking not just a personal habit, but a civic responsibility.

Take a meme that screams, *"Youth voter turnout is at an all-time low — democracy is doomed!"* It looks convincing with numbers and graphics, but where did those stats come from? If the source isn't clear, that's a red flag. Before sharing, check official data from trusted organizations like the Census Bureau or a reputable research center. Compare the numbers. If they don't match, you've just stopped misinformation in its tracks.

Headlines thrive on drama too. *"The End of Democracy Is Here!"* might sound urgent, but is it? Click through. Does the article cite experts and provide context, or is it built on speculation? If you're still unsure, consult multiple credible outlets or use a fact-checking resource to cross-check. The principle is simple: don't rely on one source alone.

Images and videos can also mislead. Deepfakes and manipulated photos slip into feeds, especially during elections. If something looks odd, try a reverse image search to find the original. Watch for mismatched shadows, awkward-looking hands, or captions that don't fit.

When checking facts, transparency is key. Reliable sources explain where their information comes from and link to the evidence. Good habits aren't about perfection; they're about slowing down enough to ask: *Does this claim name a source? Can I find it on an official site? Do multiple reputable outlets report the same story?*

If you ever feel overwhelmed, remember you're not alone. Information overload is real, and it's designed to wear people down. But slowing the scroll, even just a little, protects you from spreading confusion.

Fact-checking isn't about catching every falsehood. It's about refusing to be played. It gives you the confidence to speak up and trust that your voice is grounded in truth — one of the most important building blocks of democracy itself.

Chapter 3: Threats in the Now: Spotting the Real Problems (and What's Just Noise)

"Those who can make you believe absurdities can make you commit atrocities." — Voltaire

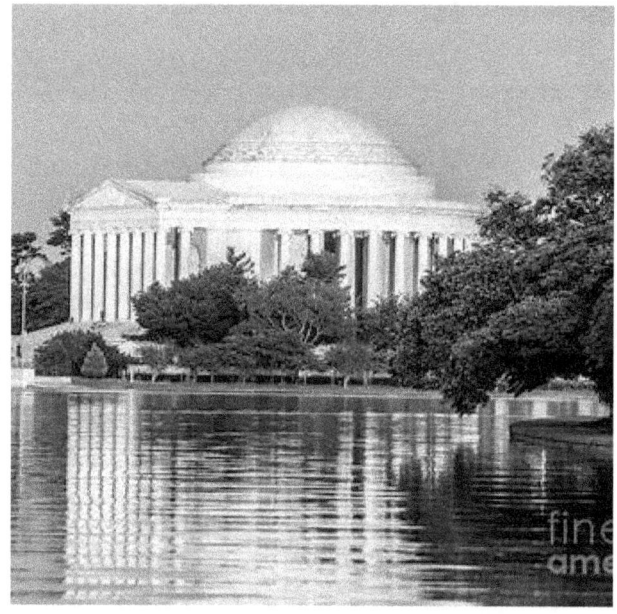

Figure 4. Jefferson Memorial, Washington, D.C. (Public Domain).

The last chapter was named Fog. This one helps you see through it. Democracies face genuine threats, but not every headline is a five-alarm fire. Therefore, learning to distinguish real danger from background noise matters so much.

We'll focus on patterns you can recognize and respond to without panic:

- How modern authoritarians test boundaries, then normalize the breach.
- How engagement algorithms distort attention and reward outrage.
- How networked disinformation spreads and how to slow it down.
- What democratic backsliding looks like step by step.
- Why is polarization profitable and how to resist being drafted into it.
- Why are so many young people tuning out, and what does it mean for the future?

The point isn't the catastrophe. Democracies have survived serious shocks before, and they can again. The goal here is pattern recognition, practical defenses, and small moves that add up. Each section ends with a brief "Try this" a concrete step you can take in your own life.

How to read this chapter: skim the overview, then dive into the sections most relevant to you. Keep an eye out for the recurring questions: What are they trying to make you believe? What's my countermove? What can my group do together?

Modern Authoritarians: How Elected Leaders Undermine Democracy

When most people picture a threat to democracy, they imagine tanks in the streets or a dictator seizing power overnight. But today it rarely looks like that. Modern authoritarians don't need dramatic coups. They use the system itself — courts, laws, elections — to slowly weaken democracy from the inside.

These "elected authoritarians" give speeches about freedom and fairness. They wave flags and smile for the cameras. And then, once in power, they start bending the rules just enough to lock in their advantage. It's not one big move. It's dozens of slight adjustments and procedural tweaks that pile up until opposition voices are muted and actual choices vanish.

Take Viktor Orbán in Hungary. He didn't arrive with soldiers; he was voted in. But once there, he stacked the courts with loyalists, rewrote election laws, and redrew voting districts. On paper, Hungary still held elections. In practice, critics say the system was rigged, so his party almost always won.

Or look at Turkey under Recep Tayyip Erdoğan. Early on, he promised reform and openness. But over time, independent newspapers were squeezed out, reporters harassed, and media outlets taken over by government allies. People still had access to news, but much of it was filtered or censored. The press stopped being a watchdog and became a guard for those in power.

What makes this playbook effective is its normalcy. Each change comes with an excuse: *"We're modernizing the courts." "We're making voting more efficient." "We're protecting the country from fake news."* Because nothing happens all at once, outrage fades into shrugs. By the time people realize what's happening, the damage is already done.

And while these examples may feel distant, the same logic can appear closer to home. Maybe a city council cuts public comment time in half. Maybe meeting notices go up at the last minute. Or maybe new rules make it harder for independent candidates to get on the ballot. None of these looks dramatic on its own. But together, they shrink participation and concentrate on power.

The danger isn't always in headline-grabbing scandals. It's in the slow drip of changes that seem ordinary, even dull — the political version of *death by a thousand cuts*. Each step might look like a technical fix or harmless change, but stacked together, they hollow out democracy until it exists in name only.

What are they trying to make you believe? Incremental rule-bending that normalizes unfair advantage.

What's the countermove? Spotting patterns early, calling out small shifts before they accumulate, and insisting on transparency even when the changes seem boring.

See Appendix F: Vigilance in Action for a practical checklist to help you track and respond to these warning signs

Social Media Algorithms and the "Echo Chamber" Trap

It feels good to be surrounded by people who agree with you. Algorithms know that. They feed us posts, videos, and headlines that confirm what we already believe. It feels safe, even energizing like being cheered on by a crowd that always takes your side.

But that safety has a cost. When disagreement gets filtered out, our sense of reality narrows. We believe everyone thinks the way we do. That's how misinformation gains traction — not because echo chambers invent falsehoods, but because they make it easier for bad information to spread unchecked.

This isn't limited to any one platform or app. Whether it's a news feed, a group chat, or a video algorithm, the pattern is the same: what gets rewarded is engagement, not accuracy. And outrage engages. A calm headline rarely travels as far or as fast as one that sparks anger or fear.

What are they trying to make you believe? Systems that reward outrage and filter out disagreement, creating closed loops where false or misleading information can circulate freely.

What's the countermove? Curate your own diversity. Follow at least a few credible voices you don't always agree with. Pause before sharing, especially if a post triggers a powerful reaction. Ask: *Who benefits if I believe this?* These small habits break the loop and slow the spread.

Disinformation 101: How Falsehoods Spread

Disinformation isn't about facts; it's about emotions. The people behind it know how to bypass logic and go straight for the gut. That's why a viral post doesn't need airtight evidence; it just needs to make you feel something fast.

Picture a meme draped in patriotic colors with a bold claim: *"Real Americans do this."* Before you process the words, the visuals stir pride or fear. You react first, think later. That's the hook.

Familiarity does the next job. The post reappears, reshared by a friend you trust. Later, it pops up again in a different outfit: a short video, a screenshot with snappy commentary. The more often you see it, the more familiar it feels. And familiarity often passes for truth.

The messenger adds weight. Disinformation spreads best when it looks like it comes to someone credible: a family member in a group chat, an influencer with a big following, or a stranger styling themselves "Dr." or "Professor." Whether those credentials are real, the appearance of authority makes the claim harder to doubt.

Even skeptics get fooled. Clever editing and synthetic media can make a public figure appear to say something outrageous they never said.

Cropped or context-stripped photos mislead just as effectively. Our brains take shortcuts: if something looks polished or arrives from a trusted source, we're more likely to accept it without digging.

Then come the amplifiers. Automated accounts can like, share, and flood timelines so fringe content looks popular. Coordinated troll networks seed the same talking points across comment sections and forums to manufacture consensus — or to pick fights that boost visibility. Together, these tactics make lies look bigger and more mainstream than they are.

This isn't abstract. During elections around the world, coordinated campaigns have targeted immigrant communities, spread false voting instructions, and amplified divisive narratives to sow distrust. Falsehoods often move fastest in private channels, encrypted group chats or neighborhood threads where fact-checkers and journalists can't easily follow.

So how do you protect yourself and your circles? Start with a deliberate pause. Before you share, run a quick, repeatable check:

- Who's the source? Can you trace their credibility beyond a username or bio?
- What's the evidence? Are there links to data, documents, or primary reporting?
- Is it current? Could this be an old story recycled for outrage?
- Can you cross-verify? Do multiple credible outlets report the same thing?
- Does it look manipulated? If it's an image or video, try a quick reverse image search and look for oddities (mismatched shadows, distorted hands, strange artifacts).
- What emotion is it triggering? If you feel furious, terrified, or triumphant, pause — that's often the point.
- Who benefits if this spreads? Consider the incentive behind the message.

Even a moment of hesitation can break the chain. Choosing curiosity over impulse keeps you from becoming an unknowing amplifier.

What are they trying to make you believe? Emotional manipulation amplified through repetition, borrowed (or fake) authority, synthetic visuals, and manufactured popularity — all designed to bypass critical thinking.

What's the countermove? Slow the scroll. Verify before you share. Diversify what you read and whom you follow. Treat high-emotion claims with extra skepticism. Share only what you can source, protecting not just your own judgment, but your community's trust.

Warning Signs: How Democracies Slip Toward Authoritarianism

Democratic erosion often arrives quietly. Rules change a little at a time. Norms are bent, then broken, then treated as normal. The story is rarely about a single dramatic moment. It is a series of small shifts that add up.

Patterns to watch:
- Emergencies are used to justify new powers, then those powers persist after the crisis.
- Attacks on referees: courts, election officials, independent media, civil servants.
- "Just procedural" changes that tilt the field: gerrymanders, rule changes, court-packing, selective enforcement.
- Loyalists are placed in watchdog roles, while professional expertise is sidelined.
- Legal tools aimed at critics: selective lawsuits, investigations, or penalties.
- Language that paints opponents as enemies or traitors, making abuses easier to excuse.

What are they trying to make you believe? Gradual institutional capture through legal-seeming changes, expansion of emergency powers, and normalization of behavior that used to be unacceptable.

What's the countermove? Track patterns over time, not just incidents. Call out gradual changes in public. Support independent journalism and judicial oversight. Vote in all elections, especially local ones, where institutional shifts begin. Document and share evidence of concerning patterns with credible civic organizations.

Actionable vigilance looks like this:
- Keep a simple log of changes and statements with dates and sources.
- Share your log with a local newsroom or civic group when patterns emerge.
- Attend public meetings and submit comments for the record.
- Support nonpartisan election administration and open-records efforts.
- Help others register and show up for off-cycle and local elections.

Vigilance is not passive. It is steady, organized attention that turns concern into verifiable records, public pressure, and turnout.

"Us vs. Them" The Hidden Costs to Community

"Divided we fall, united we stand" is not just a saying from history books. It is a lesson every relationship teaches us. When challenges come up, the easy move is to turn away, to stop talking, to walk out of the room, to cut ties. But the stronger move, the move that changes things, is staying in the conversation long enough to work it out. The same truth applies to families, workplaces, and democracies.

Polarization does not arrive with a bang; it slips in quietly. A family dinner ends in silence because someone brings up politics. A group chat that once overflowed with jokes and memes cracks apart over one tense post.

Suddenly, a friendship frays after a single exchange of news. At first, it feels small, but the impact is real trust erodes, and people see not just opposing opinions but opposing characters. It becomes less about disagreement and more about danger.

"Us" is good. "Them" is bad.

I have watched it break down communities. Families that used to gather every holiday now split into separate celebrations. Parents in the same school district glare across board meetings instead of improving their kids' classrooms. Workplaces grow colder when colleagues stop collaborating, afraid a stray comment could spark gossip or accusations. Even volunteer groups, once bound by a shared purpose, dissolve into factions when ideological lines get drawn too deep.

Town halls are among the clearest mirrors. Instead of neighbors hashing out issues, people yell past each other, waiting for their turn to shout. Meetings meant to build solutions collapse into scorekeeping contests. The louder the division grows, the harder it becomes to remember that everyone in the room actually lives on the same streets, shops in the same stores, and sends their kids to the same schools.

Behind all this is a mental habit that social scientists call "othering." In everyday terms, it's the slide into us-versus-them thinking, turning people who disagree with us into caricatures, villains, or even enemies. History is full of grim examples. Leaders call critics "traitors" or "enemies of the people."

Groups scapegoat outsiders for every setback. Once someone is labeled "them," it's easier to dismiss their voice, ignore their pain, or justify hurting them. Democracy doesn't just weaken in those moments. It fractures.

But here's the good news: division is not destiny. Bridges can be built. The first step is humility admitting that we all carry blind spots. Instead of rushing to defend your side, ask, "What makes you feel that way?" or "Can you help me understand?" Groups like Braver Angels have proven that even fierce opponents can sit in the same room and find respect. Not agreement on every issue, but respect.

You don't need an organization to practice this in your own life. Invite someone with different views for coffee, not to argue but to listen. If your group chat explodes, suggest a face-to-face conversation rather than endless snarky replies. Volunteering side by side with someone whose politics you don't share, serving meals at a shelter or tutoring students reminds us that common ground is stronger than we think.

Even the simple act of holding space for disagreement without ending a relationship is radical right now. Every time someone chooses dialogue over silence, or curiosity over contempt, the community strengthens. And when communities strengthen, democracy regains its backbone.

The hidden cost of polarization is losing sight of each other's humanity. The hidden gift of working through it is rediscovering that we're better together than apart.

Holding the Line Together

When people talk about democracy in crisis, it's easy to picture only leaders, laws, or headlines. But the truth is, democracy lives or dies in smaller, quieter places, in how we treat neighbors, in whether we call out disinformation, whether we keep showing up even when we're discouraged. Authoritarians chip away at systems, algorithms narrow our views, disinformation clouds our judgment, polarization splits.

Communities, and young people tune out when they feel unheard. None of these threats alone can end democracy overnight. But left unchecked together, they weaken its core.

Here's the good news: the same is true in reverse. Each time a teacher makes space for honest debate in class, democracy gets stronger. Each time someone pauses before sharing a misleading meme, democracy steadies.

Every time a divided family keeps talking instead of walking away, the cracks close just a little.

When young people take the mic at city hall, or when volunteers fact-check in real time, democracy doesn't just survive; it grows.

The threats we face now are not abstract. They are happening in classrooms, feeds, workplaces, and town halls. But so are the solutions. That is the hidden power of democracy; it multiplies through ordinary actions, by people who refuse to let fear or fatigue write the story.

If the dangers of Chapter 3 teach us anything, it is this: the biggest risk isn't the noise; it is giving up. The fog clears when we stay engaged, call out the slow drip of unfairness, and keep one another accountable.

The next chapter will show how to take these insights and turn them into everyday action. Spotting the threats is only half the work. Building resilience together is where democracy takes its next breath.

Chapter 4: Digital Literacy: Tools for the Democratic Age

Without facts, you can't have truth. Without truth, you can't have trust. Without trust, we have no shared reality, no democracy." — Maria Ressa

We've just looked at the threats that weaken democratic life, from echo chambers to disinformation campaigns. Now it's time to shift focus: how can you protect yourself, your circles, and your community from those same forces?

This chapter is about digital literacy, the new civic literacy. In today's world, the ability to spot manipulation, question sources, and navigate information streams is as vital as casting a ballot.

Here, we'll explore practical tools you can start using right away:
- Spotting red flags that signal disinformation.
- Understanding how lies develop and why repetition makes them stick.
- Breaking out of echo chambers without losing your footing.
- Building everyday digital defense habits that strengthen not only your judgment, but your community's trust.

Think of this as your toolkit for the digital age — clear, accessible habits that anyone can practice. No jargon, no advanced course numbers. Just the skills you need to cut through the noise, slow the spread of falsehoods, and create space for truth to thrive.

Spotting Disinformation Red Flag

Not every misleading post is a deepfake or troll farm product. Often, the first warning signs are small details that don't quite line up. These "red flags" don't mean something is automatically false, but they should signal you to pause, double-check, and verify before you share.

Use this quick checklist when evaluating suspicious content:

☐ **Unclear sourcing.** No author, organization, or credible outlet attached.

☐ **Emotional triggers.** Headlines or captions designed to spark outrage, fear, or triumph.

☐ **Recycled or out-of-date content.** Old images, stories, or footage being presented as current.

☐ **Manipulated visuals.** Look for shadows or reflections that don't match, hands or ears that appear distorted, unnatural blinking or lip-syncing, or identical faces repeated in a crowd (signs of AI or heavy editing).

☐ **Awkward audio/video sync.** Words slightly mismatched with lip movement, sudden audio cuts, or background sounds that don't match the scene.

☐ **Too polished or too raw.** Both extremes can be suspected — either overproduced without attribution or "grassroots-looking" with no verifiable context.

☐ **No corroboration.** If it's true, multiple credible outlets should eventually cover it.

What are they trying to make you believe? Exploiting our shortcuts in attention — slipping falsehoods past us through emotional triggers, synthetic visuals, or repackaged old content.

What's the countermove? Treat red flags as signals, not verdicts. Pause before you share, cross-verify with trusted outlets, and use quick tools like reverse image search or fact-check sites. Protecting your community's trust starts with small moments of verification.

Appendix G: Digital Defense Checklist provides a step-by-step version of these red flags for quick use.

Disinformation 201: Building Immunity to Lies

If *Disinformation 101* was about spotting how falsehoods spread, this is about building habits that make you harder to fool. Researchers call it "inoculation," but it's less like a vaccine and more like practice drills: once you've seen the trick, you're better prepared when it shows up again.

This section highlights three areas where stronger defenses matter most: prebunking, synthetic media, and slow media habits.

Prebunking & Cognitive Resistance

Research shows that learning about manipulation techniques *before* encountering them makes them easier to resist. Think of it as mental rehearsal. Just as athletes train against likely plays from an opponent, citizens can train themselves to recognize manipulative tactics.

Common techniques to watch for:
- Fear triggers ("If you don't act, disaster will strike").
- Fake authority (claims from self-appointed "experts" with no credentials).
- Cherry-picked data (selective use of numbers or anecdotes to mislead).
- False balance (presenting fringe claims as equal to broad consensus).

What are they trying to make you believe? Exploiting surprise and unfamiliarity using manipulative moves when audiences aren't primed to recognize them.

What's the countermove? Build mental rehearsal. Expose yourself to examples of common manipulation tactics so they're easier to spot in the wild.

Deepfakes & Synthetic Media

From fabricated voices to realistic-looking videos, synthetic media can make fiction look like fact. These tools exploit our brain's shortcut: if something looks or sounds authentic, we trust it.
Red flags to watch for:
- Lighting and shadows that don't match.
- Lip-syncing slightly out of time.
- Distorted hands, ears, or background details.
- Identical faces repeated in a crowd.

What are they trying to make you believe? Using realistic but false media to erode trust, smear opponents, or create confusion.

What's the countermove? Don't assume "seeing is believing." Look for small inconsistencies, run reverse image/video searches, and rely on trusted fact-checkers before sharing.

Slow Media & Community Checking
Falsehoods thrive on speed. By the time fact-checkers weigh in, misinformation may have already gone viral. Slowing down is one of the simplest, most powerful defenses.

Practical slow media habits:
- Pause before you share, especially if the content sparks strong emotion.

- Check whether credible outlets are reporting the same story.
- Ask a trusted friend or group to help verify before amplifying.
- Normalize "wait and see" rather than racing to repost.

What are they trying to make you believe? Exploiting the viral nature of platforms to outrun corrections.
What's the countermove? Slow the spread. Build habits that prioritize accuracy over speed, and encourage your circles to fact-check together.

By practicing these habits, you don't just protect yourself; you help shield your community. Falsehoods lose power when ordinary people choose to pause, question, and verify.

Breaking the Echo Chamber: Why It Feels So Good (and So Dangerous)

Have you ever noticed how satisfying it feels when your feed agrees with you? Every article supports your perspective, every meme makes the "other side" look foolish, and every "like" feels like proof you're right.

That comfort isn't accidental. Social media platforms keep you engaged, and the easiest way to do that is by showing you more of what you already agree with. Psychologists call this confirmation bias. Our brains crave validation, and algorithms happily supply it.

But what feels reassuring can quietly become dangerous.

The Algorithm's Trap

Every time you click, pause, or comment, the algorithm takes note. It responds by showing you more of the same — and less of everything else. What begins as curiosity can spin into a closed loop where you only see one side of an issue.

The danger lies not only in what you see, but in what you don't. Balanced reporting, nuanced perspectives, and stories outside your usual worldview all get buried. Over time, your sense of reality becomes narrower, even though your feed feels full.

Why It Matters for Democracy

Democracy depends on shared facts and diverse voices. When citizens live in separate echo chambers, common ground shrinks. It becomes harder to debate policies or even agree on basic truths when people are confined to parallel realities.

At their most extreme, echo chambers don't automatically radicalize people, but they can create the conditions for radicalization. Repeated exposure, trusted messengers, and emotionally charged content can slowly turn a casual group into one where conspiracy theories or even hate take root.

How to Break Out

Escaping an echo chamber does not mean abandoning your beliefs. It means reclaiming the ability to see the bigger picture. Strategies include:
- **Add balance intentionally**. Follow at least one credible outlet outside your comfort zone. You don't need to agree — just understand.
- **Reverse the algorithm.** Click on fact-checks, long-form journalism, and quality reporting. The more you engage with truth, the more the algorithm amplifies it.

- **Research in private**. When looking up controversial topics, use an incognito or private window to avoid being funneled by your own search history.
- **Step offline. Real** conversations with neighbors, coworkers, or classmates often reveal more nuance than any curated feed.

What are they trying to make you believe? Algorithmic amplification of agreeable content while filtering out challenging perspectives, creating false consensus and informational isolation.

What's the countermove? Intentionally diversify your information sources. Follow credible outlets outside your comfort zone, use private browsing for research, and prioritize face-to-face conversations over curated feeds.

Comfort vs. Truth

Echo chambers feel good because they make the world simple. But democracy doesn't thrive on comfort — it thrives on dialogue, disagreement, and discovery.

Breaking out of your bubble may feel uncomfortable at first, but it's also liberating. It reconnects you with the wider reality and restores your role as an active citizen, not just a consumer of algorithm-curated outrage.

Breaking Out of Echo Chambers

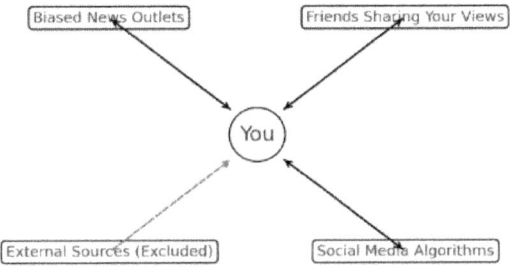

Figure 5: How echo chambers isolate you from outside perspectives. (Author Created)

Tools for Everyday Digital Defense

There isn't a single app that can "truth-proof" your feed. Tools change. Principles last. The goal here isn't to memorize products — it's to practice habits that travel with you across platforms.

Use these durable checks:

☐ **Read laterally.** Open a new tab and see how multiple credible outlets cover the same claim. Look for bylines, sourcing, and whether others can corroborate.

☐ **Trace to the source.** Follow quotes, screenshots, and stats back to an original document, full video, or primary reporting. Summaries and memes often drop key context.

☐ **Check timing and context.** Verify dates, locations, and whether old footage is being presented as new. Be cautious with dramatic "breaking" posts that lack details.

☐ **Verify visuals.** Use any reverse image or reverse video search you prefer. Scan for reuse of the same image elsewhere and for inconsistencies (lighting, reflections, lip sync).

☐ **Compare coverage.** Look at local reporting, specialist outlets, and a range of credible perspectives. If a story is true and important, independent confirmation should emerge.

☐ **Mind the emotions.** Outrage and triumph are attention magnets. When a post spikes your feelings, pause and recheck before you share.

☐ **Step outside the feed.** For research, use private/incognito windows or a different browser profile to reduce personalization. Balance feeds with newsletters, podcasts, or print that you curate yourself.

☐ **Use the "two-person rule."** Before amplifying a hot claim, ask one trusted friend to sense-check it. Community verification beats speed.

☐ **Share corrections with care.** If you amplified something wrong, post a clear update with a source. Model the behavior you want in your circles.

Note: Fact-checking sites and browser "trust" signals can help, but they're not infallible. Treat them as inputs to your judgment, not substitutes for it.

What are they trying to make you believe? Overloading attention and exploiting personalization so emotionally charged, low-context content outruns verification.

What's the countermove? Slow the spread and set a higher standard: read laterally, trace to sources, verify visuals, compare coverage, and recruit a second set of eyes before you share. Tools can assist, but disciplined habits do genuine work.

Digital literacy isn't about knowing everything. It's about knowing where to look, how to check, and when to pause. That is how everyday citizens become everyday defenders of democracy.

Chapter 5: Real People, Real Change: Stories and Lessons from Everyday Democracy

"The salvation of this human world lies nowhere else than in the human heart, in the human power to reflect, in human meekness and human responsibility." — Václav Havel

In the last chapter, we focused on digital defenses — the habits that help you cut through manipulation and guard community trust. Here, we turn from screens to streets, classrooms, faith halls, and dinner tables. This chapter explores how everyday people live democracy in practice.

You'll hear stories of communities that built bridges across divides, movements that grew from ordinary voices, and local heroes who refused to look away when democratic values were at stake.

Specifically, we'll look at:

- Immigrant voices expanding the democratic conversation.
- Youth movements shaping civic life with fresh energy.
- Women and faith communities stepping into leadership roles.
- Local heroes who stood up for fairness and accountability.
- Dialogue across differences, including in families and neighborhoods.

This is not a story about perfection. It's about persistence. Building trust in divided communities, engaging without burning out, and taking small, practical steps, these are possible when citizens recognize their own agency.

By the end of this chapter, you'll see democracy not as an abstract ideal but as something alive in ordinary lives, including your own.

Immigrant Voices: Expanding the Democratic Conversation

"What we need to realize is that our democracy is stronger when more voices are included, not fewer." — Ilhan Omar

If you've ever thought democracy only happens on television or at city hall, immigrant stories will prove otherwise. In countless neighborhoods across the country, democracy is alive in church basements, school gyms, corner cafés, and library meeting rooms often thanks to the energy of people who weren't born here but built here.

Consider recent campaigns in cities like New York and San Francisco, where immigrant coalitions have successfully pushed for multilingual ballot guides and translation services at polling places. These changes weren't just about convenience; they meant entire neighborhoods could finally participate with confidence.

Across the country, immigrant-led groups have organized *Know Your Rights* workshops, legal clinics, and neighborhood associations. In Minneapolis, Latino business owners rallied for fair licensing rules. In Maine, Somali Bantu farmers formed a cooperative that gave them both economic independence and a political voice. These stories vary, but the thread is consistent: civic participation grows when immigrants lead.

It's important to acknowledge, though, that immigrant civic engagement isn't uniform. Legal status, economic pressures, language access, and community support all shape how and whether people can get involved. Not every immigrant community has the same resources, but when barriers are lowered, participation rises.

What these examples reveal is simple but powerful: immigrants don't just adapt to democracy, they expand it. They remind us that democracy is not a finished system; it's an ongoing project that grows stronger every time a fresh voice joins in.

What are they trying to make you believe? Framing immigrants as outsiders, unqualified to shape policy, or unworthy of a political voice.

What's the countermove? Recognize the democratic insights immigrants bring. Support inclusive policies, push for language access, and amplify immigrant-led organizations already building civic power.

Reflection: Amplifying Immigrant Voices in Your World
Look around your school, workplace, or town. Whose stories aren't heard? If you know someone who speaks another language or comes from another country, ask about their experiences with voting, public meetings, or local news. Offer to share their story, invite them into a project, or if you can, lend your skills as an interpreter or translator. Every time an immigrant voice is amplified, democracy gets a little more resilient and a lot more real.

The courage of immigrant communities shows how democracy expands when more voices are welcomed to the table. That same spirit of renewal is also visible in the next generation — young people who are refusing to wait their turn to lead.

Youth at the Forefront of Democracy: The Power of Student Movements

"Young people are not the leaders of tomorrow — they are the leaders of today."
— Kailash Satyarthi, Nobel Peace Prize laureate

Young people are often dismissed as "too idealistic" or "too inexperienced." Yet throughout history, youth have been among the first to demand change and to organize for it. Their perspective is shaped by urgency: they will live longest with the consequences of today's choices.

In 2018, after the mass shooting at Marjory Stoneman Douglas High School in Parkland, Florida, students organized rallies, pressed lawmakers, and launched the March for Our Lives movement. Within months, they were speaking at town halls, registering voters, and pushing gun violence prevention into the national spotlight. Their efforts contributed to the highest youth turnout in a midterm election in decades.

Another example is the Sunrise Movement, a youth-led climate justice network. What began with sit-ins at congressional offices grew into a national campaign that helped put climate policy on the political agenda. They didn't always win their demands, but they shifted the conversation — showing how persistence, creativity, and moral clarity can change what issues get taken seriously.

It's not that youth are uniquely hopeful while adults are cynical. Each generation brings different strengths.

Youth often bring energy, creativity, and a willingness to challenge norms.

Older generations often bring resources, networks, and lived experience.

When they work together, movements gain both momentum and staying power.

What are they trying to make you believe? Undermining youth participation by labeling youthful voices as naïve, dismissing their activism as performative, or making civic spaces difficult for them to access.

What's the countermove? Value intergenerational collaboration. Create pathways for young leaders to be heard, and pair their urgency with the experience and networks of older allies. Support youth-led organizations not as "future leaders" but as leaders already shaping today's democracy.

The lesson is clear: leadership is not defined by age but by action. And while young people push boundaries, women across the world continue to prove that democratic change often starts with those who have long been underestimated.

Women on the Frontlines of Democracy

"I raise up my voice — not so I can shout, but so that those without a voice can be heard." — Malala Yousafzai

For centuries, women were systematically excluded from formal democracy. Legal codes, property laws, and cultural expectations closed off voting booths, juries, and public office. Not all women resisted these restrictions, but those who did forced open doors that had long been locked. Suffragists didn't just demand ballots for themselves; they transformed the meaning of citizenship by insisting that democracy must stretch to include voices it once ignored. Women's leadership has often been powerful but under-recognized. At the 1963 March on Washington, Dorothy Height and other women mobilized thousands of participants, yet none were invited to speak on the main stage. This tension — women as organizers but not always visible leaders — shows both the persistence of barriers and the resilience of women's civic work.

That legacy continues today. In Liberia, the women's peace movement helped end a brutal civil war and pressured leaders toward democratic reforms. In Pakistan, Malala Yousafzai has become a global symbol for the fight for girls' education, reminding the world that democracy depends on equal access to knowledge and opportunity.

Closer to home, women in the United States have built coalitions to improve maternal healthcare, push for paid family leave, and protect voting rights. Groups like *Mothers of the Movement* — Black women who lost children to police violence — have turned personal tragedy into civic advocacy, pressing lawmakers to confront issues of justice and accountability.

These stories show the complexity of women's democratic contributions: they are neither accidental participants nor flawless heroes, but persistent actors who wide civic life through courage, organization, and long-term commitment.

What are they trying to make you believe? Treating women's contributions as secondary, minimizing their leadership, or excluding them from decision-making spaces.

What's the countermove? Recognize and support women's leadership at every level. Elevate women's voices in civic processes, invest in women-led organizations, and rewrite narratives that sideline women's impact.

Reflection: Where Do Women Lead Around You?
Think about your own circle. Who are the women — mothers, sisters, teachers, organizers — who push conversations forward, even when it's hard? Notice their work, thank them, or join them. If you're a woman reading this, consider one space where your voice could add a perspective that's missing. Democracy grows stronger every time women's voices are heard, amplified, and taken seriously.

Women's organizing demonstrates how everyday courage can bend the arc of history. In many places, faith communities provide the same foundation, becoming unlikely but powerful spaces where citizens gather, question, and act together.

Figure 10: Women were active participants in the March on Washington, but their leadership was sidelined. Dorothy Height, a key organizer, was excluded from speaking — a reminder that women's contributions to democracy have often been powerful but under-recognized.

Faith Communities and Democracy

"Faith is taking the first step even when you don't see the whole staircase." — Martin Luther King Jr.

Faith communities are not monolithic. At times, religion has been used to exclude or divide. But at their best, faith communities have provided spaces for courage, moral language, and collective action that strengthen democracy.

During the U.S. civil rights movement, the Black church became a base for organizing marches, sustaining hope, and articulating a vision of justice rooted in shared values. In Poland during the 1980s, the Catholic Church provided shelter and support for the Solidarity movement, helping citizens push back against authoritarian rule. And today, interfaith coalitions across Europe and the U.S. work together on refugee resettlement, showing how religious communities can extend democratic values of welcome and participation.

Not every congregation leans toward democracy, and some have been co-opted for partisan ends. But the examples above show how faith spaces — when open and inclusive — can nurture trust, solidarity, and civic courage.

What are they trying to make you believe? Exploiting religious identity to divide citizens, co-opting faith traditions for partisan gain, or silencing dissenting voices within faith communities.

What's the countermove? Support faith groups that model inclusivity and civic responsibility. Highlight traditions that protect pluralism and human dignity. Build bridges through interfaith coalitions that turn moral conviction into democratic action.

Reflection: Where Does Faith Inspire Civic Life Around You?
Think about a faith group in your community a church, mosque, synagogue, temple, or interfaith coalition. How have they shaped public conversations or supported civic life? If you're part of a congregation, what role could it play in building bridges or defending fairness?

Whether in mosques, churches, or temples, faith groups remind us that democracy is lived out in community. The same lesson holds true in neighborhoods everywhere, where local heroes show that small acts of courage can have an outsized impact.

Local Heroes: Everyday People Defending Democracy

Democracy moves not only forward in legislatures or courtrooms. Often, it's advanced by ordinary people in ordinary places who refuse to look away when fairness is threatened.

Consider Ruby Bridges, the six-year-old who in 1960 became the first Black child to integrate an all-white elementary school in New Orleans. Her bravery in walking past jeering crowds just to enter a classroom forced her city, and her country, to confront the hypocrisy of segregation. Her actions as a child became a catalyst for broader change.

Or take the librarians who, in recent years, have resisted efforts to ban books from public shelves. In Llano County, Texas, librarians and residents fought back against political pressure to remove titles on race and LGBTQ issues. Their advocacy not only preserved access to diverse books but also affirmed the role of public institutions in serving every citizen.

Poll workers are another example of unsung heroes. In Georgia, organizers like Wanda Mosley and her colleagues at Fair Fight recruited, trained, and protected thousands of volunteers to ensure fair access to the ballot. Their vigilance in local precincts helped safeguard elections under intense scrutiny.

These stories remind us that local action matters. Democracy is not an abstract ideal; it is lived out in classrooms, libraries, and polling places where ordinary people choose courage over silence.

What are they trying to make you believe? Dismissing or undermining local efforts by portraying them as insignificant, partisan, or disruptive.

What's the countermove? Celebrate and support local democratic action. Recognize that small acts of teaching, protecting access, defending fairness ripple outward into broader democratic resilience.

Reflection: Who Are the Local Heroes Around You?
Think about your own community. Is there a teacher, librarian, organizer, or neighbor who has stood up for fairness or inclusion? How can you acknowledge their work by thanking them, joining them, or sharing their story with others?

Local heroes prove that democracy is not the work of distant institutions, but of neighbors and families. And it is in those closest relationships across divides of politics, race, or class where the hardest and most necessary work of democracy takes place.

Bridging Divides: Dialogue Across Differences

"Being heard is so close to being loved that for the average person they are almost indistinguishable." — David Augsburger

Polarization thrives when neighbors stop talking and opponents see each other only as enemies. Across the country, groups are proving that dialogue can bridge divides not by erasing differences, but by creating spaces where disagreement coexists with respect.

One example is Braver Angels, a grassroots movement launched after the 2016 U.S. election. Its workshops bring conservatives, progressives, and independents together to share personal stories, listen without interruption, and seek common values. Evaluations of these workshops show participants often leave with lower animosity even if their views don't change.

Another model is Living Room Conversations, where small groups gather at home or online to discuss topics like immigration or policing. Ground rules are simple: respect, equal time, and no "winning." These conversations don't end polarization, but they do humanize it.

What are they trying to make you believe? Exploiting polarization by portraying opponents as irredeemable enemies and fueling outrage over understanding.

What's the countermove? Build structured spaces for dialogue. Support organizations that normalize respectful conversation, and model discussions that are honest, curious, and grounded in shared dignity.

Reflection: Where Could You Build Dialogue?
Think about a space in your life — work, a neighborhood group, your extended family — where disagreement flares. What would it take to set ground rules and invite a conversation across difference?

Bridging divides shows that democracy is sustained not by agreement on every issue, but by the willingness to stay in relationship across disagreement. The same principle applies in our most personal spaces, including around the dinner table.

Democracy at the Dinner Table

"Most people do not listen with the intent to understand; they listen with the intent to reply." — Stephen R. Covey

The dinner table may not seem like a civic space, but it often functions as one of the first places we learn how to disagree. Here, children watch adults model listening or shouting. They absorb whether questions are welcomed or silenced, whether curiosity is encouraged or mocked.

Research from **Harvard's Making Caring Common Project** shows that family discussions about current events and values are linked to stronger civic engagement in young people.

It's not about everyone holding the same views — it's about learning to argue without contempt and to listen without surrendering your beliefs.
Some families establish *"civic rituals"* — choosing one news story each week to discuss, inviting children to explain their perspectives, or rotating who picks the topic.
Others practice *"structured disagreement"* — where each person takes a turn stating their view while others listen before responding.

These habits don't end polarization, but they prepare the next generation with democratic skills that travel far beyond the table.

What are they trying to make you believe?
That your home should be a zone of silence or hostility where young people never practice democratic dialogue.

What's the countermove? Use family and community meals as practice grounds for democracy. Model respect, curiosity, and disagreement without contempt. Treat the dinner table as training for the public square.

Reflection: How Democratic Is Your Dinner Table?
Think back to your last few meals with family or friends. Did everyone have a chance to speak? Were questions encouraged or avoided? What one change could make your table a space where listening and respect grow?

The dinner table may seem small, but it shapes the habits that ripple outward into schools, workplaces, and neighborhoods. And those everyday habits prepare citizens to act with courage and respect in larger democratic spaces.

Heroes of Everyday Democracy

"Give light and people will find the way." — Ella Baker

Not all democratic heroes hold office or make headlines. Many are neighbors whose persistence quietly reshapes civic life.

In Flint, Michigan, **LeeAnne Walters**, a mother worried about her children's rashes, pushed for answers about brown, foul-smelling tap water. She organized testing, teamed with scientists and doctors, and helped expose systemic failures that endangered an entire city.

Walters worked closely with **Dr. Marc Edwards**, a civil engineer from Virginia Tech, and **Dr. Mona Hanna-Attisha**, a pediatrician who revealed elevated lead levels in children's blood.

National media figures like **Rachel Maddow** helped amplify their voices, bringing urgent attention to a crisis that local officials had downplayed.

One mother's tenacity, backed by science, medicine, and media, helped force accountability. A reminder that **democracy begins at the tap.**

In Atlanta, Georgia, **election workers Ruby Freeman and Shaye Moss** kept ballots moving on election night — then endured a wave of harassment stoked by false claims.

Their names and lives were dragged into conspiracy theories promoted by political operatives and media figures. Despite the threats, they stood their ground, told the truth publicly, and later testified before Congress with courage and clarity.

Their truth-telling helped lead to **landmark defamation judgments** and inspired wider efforts to protect election workers nationwide.

Their courage and the support of those who stood with them affirmed ordinary people can **defend the machinery of free and fair elections**.

In Brooklyn, neighbors formed Bed-Stuy Strong, a mutual-aid network that mobilized volunteers to deliver groceries and essentials during the pandemic, redirecting community donations to tens of thousands of households. Civic care scaled into civic power.

These stories remind us that democracy is not an abstraction — it's sustained by ordinary people who choose responsibility over resignation.

What are they trying to make you believe? Erasing or belittling grassroots actors by crediting only elites or institutions, or by dismissing a local action as "not political."

What's the countermove? Center everyday citizens in our democratic story. Celebrate local courage, replicate practical models, and remember that structural change rests on daily, distributed effort.

Reflection: Who Are the Everyday Heroes Around You?
Name one person whose steady actions made your community fairer or kinder. How could you support, learn from, or join them this month?

Chapter 6: Everyday Actions: Your Personal Democracy Toolkit

"The ballot is stronger than the bullet." — Abraham Lincoln

This chapter is your toolkit — a set of practical, customizable ways to bring democracy into your daily life. Not every tool will fit your schedule, skills, or comfort level, and that's okay. Think of this as a menu, not a mandate: you can pick and choose, experiment, and return to what works best for you.

Inside, you'll find:

- A Civic Action Plan to help you set sustainable goals.
- Micro-actions you can do in five minutes a day.
- Ways to volunteer beyond elections so your impact lasts year-round.
- Guidance for hosting or joining digital town halls.
- A bridge-building template for tough conversations.
- Tips for making public comments that get results.

Democracy isn't about heroic bursts of energy; it's about steady participation that fits into real lives. Whether you have five minutes, five hours, or five days, this chapter will give you tools to make your contribution practical and sustainable.

Your Civic Action Plan: Personalizing Participation for Your Life

When it comes to civic engagement, there's no single "right" way to contribute. What matters is finding a sustainable rhythm that works for you, one that avoids burnout and builds long-term commitment.

Start by asking yourself three guiding questions:
1. What issues matter to me most?
2. How much time and energy can I realistically give?
3. What strengths or skills do I bring to the table?

From these answers, you can sketch out your personal Civic Action Plan.

Think of it like a ladder:
- The first rung might be simple steps such as signing a petition or subscribing to a credible newsletter.
- The next rung could involve joining a local meeting or volunteering for a community project.
- Higher rungs might include organizing an event, leading a campaign, or mentoring others.

Each rung builds on the last. You don't have to climb the whole ladder at once. Start where you are, move up when you're ready, and remember that consistency matters more than heroics.

What are they trying to make you believe? Making civic life seem overwhelming or inaccessible, so people feel powerless and opt out entirely.

What's the countermove? Break the engagement into manageable steps. Choose actions that align with your interests, skills, and time, and build upward at your own pace.

Reflection: Your Civic Action Ladder
Sketch a quick version of your own ladder on paper. What's one small action you can take this week? What's one bigger step you could aim for in the next three months?

Micro-Actions with Macro Impact: Democracy in Five Minutes a Day

Not everyone can attend weekly meetings or organize rallies. But democracy isn't built only in big bursts; it's also strengthened by small, steady actions. In just a few minutes a day, you can reinforce civic trust, broaden conversations, and push back against misinformation.

Here are examples of five-minute actions that add up over time:
- Share a credible fact-check when you see misinformation circulating.
- Email or call a local representative about one issue that matters to you.
- Register for election reminders so you never miss a vote.
- Read one article from a news outlet outside your usual circle.
- Thank a poll worker, teacher, or librarian for their service.

Some readers find it motivating to gamify these actions. Imagine a "Democracy Bingo" card with squares like *attend a school board meeting, support local journalism,* or *talk politics respectfully with a neighbor.* As you complete actions, check off squares until you hit "Bingo." Others use a Democracy Tracker, a simple calendar where you mark small daily actions to see progress build. (Sample templates are included in the appendix.)

These habits prove you don't need hours of free time to make a difference. What matters is showing up consistently, even in bite-sized ways.

What are they trying to make you believe? Convincing people that democracy requires extraordinary time, knowledge, or sacrifice — creating paralysis through perfectionism.

What's the countermove? Normalize micro-actions as real contributions. Show that even five minutes, repeated often, helps defend civic life.

Reflection: Five Minutes for Democracy.
What's one five-minute action you could add to your week? Write it down, try it for a month, and notice how it changes your sense of connection and agency.

Appendix C includes a printable Democracy Tracker and Five-Minute Democracy Bingo card to make these actions more visible and fun

Volunteering Beyond Elections: Year-Round Opportunities for Change

Democracy doesn't begin and end on Election Day. The health of our communities depends on steady, year-round participation, and some of the most meaningful opportunities to serve are found outside the voting booth.

Here are some ways to plug in:
- Support basic needs. Volunteer at a local food bank, community fridge, or housing nonprofit. Meeting immediate needs builds trust that strengthens civic life.
- Court-watch and observe. Many cities have court-watching programs where citizens attend proceedings to ensure fairness and transparency in the justice system.
- Mentor and tutor. Schools and after-school programs need adults to support students with reading, math, or life skills. Investing in young people is investing in democracy's future.
- Join a civic group. Organizations like the League of Women Voters, AmeriCorps, and local advocacy groups provide structured ways to learn, connect, and act.

- Engage with the local government. Volunteer for a commission, advisory board, or neighborhood council. These small bodies shape policies that ripple outward.

These roles rarely make headlines, but they add up. They build relationships, strengthen institutions, and remind us that democracy is a practice we carry forward together.

What are they trying to make you believe? Treating civic engagement as something that matters only during elections and leaving public life to professional politicians the rest of the year.

What's the countermove? Volunteer consistently, even in small ways, throughout the year. Connect with organizations that sustain civic health beyond the ballot box.

Reflection: Beyond November
Think about one issue you care about most — food security, schools, housing, justice. What's one volunteer opportunity you could explore in the next month? Write down a commitment, however small, and share it with a friend to keep yourself accountable.

Grassroots Organizing: Building from the Ground Up

Sometimes change requires more than individual action — it takes collective effort. Grassroots organizing helps neighbors, coworkers, and community members come together with a purpose.

Here's how to start small and build momentum:
- Create a shared document for tasks and supplies.
- Use a group chat to keep everyone informed.
- Set one specific goal: pick up litter that fills 20 bags, plant 10 trees, or gather 30 signatures for a safer crosswalk.
- Assign roles so people show up confidently.

Your first meeting can be four people in a living room or on Zoom. Agenda: the problem, the goal, who does what, next steps, and next date. Celebrate small wins. Momentum is built on victories, not just effort.

Tell the story. Share why the issue matters. Add before-and-after photos, short videos, or simple flyers. People rally when they see both the problem and the possibility.

Be inclusive. Translate flyers, make the space accessible, invite newcomers, elders, and quieter voices. When everyone sees themselves reflected, the movement grows.

What are they trying to make you believe? Making people believe only large institutions can drive change.

What's the countermove? Show how small groups can self-organize with structure, inclusivity, and storytelling to build momentum.

Reflection: Organizing in Your World
What's one issue in your neighborhood that a handful of people could tackle together? Write three people you could invite into a group chat or living-room meeting to get started.

Digital Town Halls: Hosting and Participating Online with Impact

Community meetings don't have to happen in school gyms anymore. Digital platforms make it easier to gather people across neighborhoods or time zones.

Here are a few practices to make them effective:

- Accessibility matters. Use captions, provide materials in advance, and schedule across time zones when possible.
- Keep it simple. Choose tools your audience already knows. A Zoom poll or chat box can be just as effective as specialized apps.
- Moderate actively. Assign someone to track questions, watch the chat, and keep time.
- Invite broadly. Share links widely, not just with insiders. Use newsletters, social media, or flyers so fresh voices are included.
- Follow up. Summarize decisions and next steps in writing within 24 hours so accountability doesn't fade.

What are they trying to make you believe? Turning digital spaces into echo chambers or exclusive circles, where only a few voices dominate.

What's the countermove? Make online meetings inclusive, structured, and accessible. Treat digital town halls as open doors, not gated communities.

Reflection: Hosting Your Own Digital Town Hall
If you wanted to gather 10 people on an issue that matters to you, what platform would you use? Which one practice above (captions, follow-up notes, broad invites) would make it more inclusive?

Public Comment That Gets Results: Emails, Calls, and 60-Second Testimony

Public officials make decisions every day but only hear from a fraction of the people affected. Thoughtful public comment is one of the simplest and most powerful ways to shape policy.

Use the **P.E.A.R. framework** to guide your message:

- **Personalize.** Say who you are and why this issue matters to you. Example: "As a parent with two children in the district, I've seen how library programs help kids thrive."
- **Evidence.** Add one fact, statistic, or real-world example to back up your point. Keep it short but credible.
- **Ask.** Make a straightforward request for action: "Please support increased funding for school libraries in the upcoming budget."
- **Respect.** Thank the official for their time or service, and keep your tone civil — even if you strongly disagree.

Emails
- Keep it to 3–4 short paragraphs.
- Use a clear subject line: "Support funding for local libraries."
- End with a thank you and your contact information.

Calls
- Prepare a two-sentence script: "I'm a resident of [city]. I'm calling to urge you to support [specific action]. Thank you for your service."
- Be brief and respectful — staffers often log dozens of calls a day.

Testimony (in person or online)
- Focus on 60 seconds.
- Lead with your personal connection, back it up with one fact, and close with your ask.
- Practice once aloud so you stay within the time limit.

What are they trying to make you believe? Let apathy or intimidation keep citizens silent, leaving decision-making to a few loud voices.

What's the countermove? Use clear, respectful, repeatable formats like the P.E.A.R. framework to make your voice heard in every channel.

Reflection: One Comment This Month

Pick one issue that matters to you. Draft a short email or call script using P.E.A.R. and send it this week. Notice how it feels to move from silence to action.

Chapter 7: Building Resilience: Community Strength in a Polarized World

"Never doubt that a small group of thoughtful, committed citizens can change the world; indeed, it is the only thing that ever has."
— Margaret Mead

Hope can feel fragile these days. Between constant news of crises, political division, and the exhausting pace of modern life, it is easy to slip into cynicism and think, *"What is the point?"* Yet history and everyday life tell another story. When people come together with even a little hope, they rebuild towns after disasters, push through reforms once thought impossible, and remind one another that community is stronger than fear.

This chapter is not about blind optimism. It is about active hope—the kind that rolls up its sleeves and shows up in both ordinary and extraordinary ways. Resilient communities are not built on slogans; they are built on neighbors checking in, volunteers organizing food drives, students leading climate marches, and everyday people refusing to give up on each other.

Here we will see how resilience takes root in daily life—how trust, solidarity, and shared action give democracy its heartbeat. From neighborhood networks to international movements, the examples that follow show how ordinary people push back against despair and create spaces where democracy not only survives but thrives.

Here is the truth: cynicism isolates, but hope connects. And when hope is shared, it multiplies.

Appendix E: 30-Day Civic Sprint Playbook offers a step-by-step way to turn these conversations into sustained civic action.

Resilience Starts Local: Why Strong Communities Matter

"Alone, we can do so little; together, we can do so much." — Helen Keller

When people talk about democracy, the focus is often on the national stage—Congress, elections, presidents, prime ministers. But the real heartbeat of democracy lives closer to home. Parents debated school budgets at the PTA meeting. Volunteers gather on Saturday mornings for the neighborhood clean-up. Quietly, an all-volunteer local food pantry keeps hundreds of families afloat.

Resilience starts local. When communities are strong, they create buffers against the storms of division, misinformation, and apathy. A resilient neighborhood does not wait for a distant government to swoop in; it organizes, adapts, and supports people directly. That is where democracy feels most alive—when you can see the results in the faces of the surrounding people.

Think of a small town after a flood. Before the state can send resources, neighbors open their garages, pass out blankets, and organize food drives. Or consider a city block where residents create a WhatsApp group to check on elders during heatwaves. None of this makes the front page, but it is a proof of what democracy looks like when it is *lived*, not just *voted on*.

The beauty of local resilience is that it grows stronger with every act of trust. When you know your neighbor will check on your kids after school or lend a hand in an emergency, that trust builds a foundation deeper than any policy. It teaches people that their voices matter not only because of a ballot box, but because they are part of a community that listens and responds.

What are they trying to make you believe? Wait passively for distant institutions to solve local problems.

What's the countermove? Build neighborhood trust and networks that at first, make democracy tangible in everyday life.

Reflection: Strengthen Your Local Web
Where do you already see resilience—neighbors helping neighbors, local groups tackling problems, or small wins that go unnoticed? Jot down one example. What is one small way you could contribute to that network of trust?

Strength in Numbers: Collective Action When It Matters Most

When the world feels heavy, it is easy to believe you are too small to matter. History tells a different story: powerful change often comes not from the mighty or the wealthy, but from ordinary people who stand together when it matters most. Hard times do not just test democracy—they reveal its deepest strength: collective action.

Think about the civil rights movement. Behind the landmark speeches and national headlines were high schoolers, bus riders, preachers, and parents who organized tirelessly. Their persistence—often in the face of fear and violence—led to laws that reshaped America. These stories remind us that when people act together, they can bend history toward justice.

Or picture of a neighborhood struck by disaster. The storm has passed; the power is out, and officials are nowhere to be found.

Neighbors check on elders next door, share generators, clear debris, and cook meals on gas stoves for everyone on the block. These quiet acts rarely make the evening news, but they show democracy's heartbeat: we are stronger when we do not leave anyone behind.

Around the world, the same pattern repeats. In South Africa, communities fractured by apartheid-built Truth and Reconciliation gatherings where victims and perpetrators told their stories openly. Pain was not erased, but sharing it together carved a path forward. In Taiwan, young activists launched the Sunflower Movement, occupying the legislature with laptops, posters, and livestreams. Their sit-in inspired citizens nationwide to demand more transparency and got it.

Closer to home, workers in large and small towns have joined forces to protect one another. From nurses demanding better staffing during the pandemic to grocery clerks organizing for safer workplaces, collective courage turned exhaustion into momentum. These were not just "labor disputes"; they were reminders that fairness comes when people speak in chorus, not whispers.

These stories matter because they shatter the myth that democracy is fragile by nature. Yes, it bends under pressure. But it also bounces back when people choose unity over despair. Each act of solidarity—whether marching in the streets, cleaning up after a storm, or refusing to be silent—adds a brick to the foundation that holds us all.

What are they trying to make you believe? Fragment people into isolated individuals who feel powerless.

What's the countermove? Unite voices in collective action—movements, strikes, marches—that turn private frustration into public power.

Reflection: Your Collective-Strength Story
Recall a time you saw people come together in challenging times. What do you remember most—the courage, the coordination, the relief of not being alone? What role did you play, and what could you bring next time?

Figure 10: Reaching across difference — handshake symbolizing dialogue, trust, and the shared hope that binds communities together (Author-Created).

Everyday Habits That Make Communities Stronger

Resilience is not only about bouncing back after disasters; it is about creating habits and networks that make communities stronger long before a crisis hits. Democracy thrives when neighbors can count on one another in good times and in uncertain ones.

Consider community gardens. On the surface, they are about fresh vegetables. Beneath the soil, trust grows. People of all ages and backgrounds share tools, trade recipes, and watch out for one another. When a storm or economic downturn hits, these connections become lifelines.

Resilience lives in classrooms, too. Teachers who encourage students to discuss tough issues are training the next generation to practice democratic dialogue. A high-school debate about climate policy is not just an assignment; it is a rehearsal for civic life.

Faith groups often step in as well. A church opening its doors during a wildfire or a mosque offering free meals during Ramadan shows resilience in action. It is not charity; it is a culture of care where everyone's dignity is protected.

Technology can help. Neighborhood forums, WhatsApp groups, and Slack channels let people share alerts and updates. These platforms can spread misinformation, yes, but when used wisely they knit communities tighter together. A quick post *"We're making a grocery run; does anyone need supplies?"*—turns pixels into solidarity.

The heart of resilience is practice. The more often people come together in small, everyday ways, the stronger their ability to face bigger challenges. You don't have to wait for a disaster. Hosting a potluck, attending a PTA meeting, or checking on a neighbor builds the invisible threads that hold communities steady when storms—literal or political—hit.

What are they trying to make you believe? Treat resilience as something only needed in emergencies.

What's the countermove? Practice small, daily acts of connection—potlucks, classroom debates, group chats—that strengthen the social fabric long before a crisis.

Reflection: Build Your Resilience Muscle
Choose one small act this month—start or join a street group chat, volunteer at a school event, or check on an elderly neighbor. Write it down and do it.

Facing Hard Truths Together

"Without truth, there can be no healing. Without forgiveness, there can be no future." — Desmond Tutu.

Resilient communities are not built by ignoring wounds; they are strengthened when people face hard truths together. South Africa's Truth and Reconciliation Commission (TRC) in the 1990s is a striking example. After decades of apartheid, mistrust and injustice ran deep. Instead of papering over those divides, the TRC created space for victims to tell their stories and for perpetrators to take responsibility. The process was painful and imperfect, but it showed that honesty—even when raw—could become the foundation for a more resilient democracy.

Most of us will never sit on a national commission, but the lesson applies locally: silence weakens communities, while honest dialogue strengthens them. Avoiding conflict may feel easier in the short term, but it leaves problems festering. Resilience grows when neighbors, colleagues, and families create spaces where truth can be spoken, heard, and acted upon.
Here are a few ways to apply this principle in everyday life:

Name the issue directly. Hidden problems don't disappear—they harden. Clear acknowledgment is the first step toward repair.

Make listening safe. Community forums, listening circles, or even a simple "story night" at a library can help people share experiences without fear of ridicule.

Balance accountability and care. Forgiveness without responsibility is hollow, but accountability without compassion can fracture trust. Resilience requires both.

Keep the conversation going. Healing is never a onetime event; it takes persistence and practice.

Resilience is not just about lending a hand during a storm; it is about having the courage to face what divides us. Communities that can tell the truth—and stay at the table afterward—are the ones that endure.

What are they trying to make you believe? Encourage silence or denial, leaving wounds unspoken and divisions to deepen.

What's the countermove? Practice truth-telling and accountability—naming problems clearly, listening with care, and sustaining dialogue.

Reflection: Truth in Your Community
What's one issue in your community that gets swept under the rug? Who could you invite into an honest conversation about it, and what would help make that dialogue feel safe?

Figure 11: Community members in South Africa share testimony during the Truth and Reconciliation process, symbolizing courage through collective dialogue (Author-Created).

Civic Education as a Shield

Democracy falters when citizens don't understand how it works. Cynicism grows when people feel powerless, and misinformation spreads when people don't know how to test what's true. That's why civic education is not a luxury; it's armor.

Finland offers a striking example. From elementary school onward, students learn how government works, yes, but also how to fact-check headlines, debate issues respectfully, and help shape school policies. They practice democracy, not just study it.

The results speak for themselves: Finland is consistently ranked among the most resilient countries against disinformation campaigns. Their model shows that teaching civic habits early strengthens a society's ability to resist manipulation and stay grounded in truth.

Other communities don't need a national overhaul to borrow the principle. Any school, library, or group can create similar shields: host workshops spotting false news, model respectful disagreement, or invite students into local decision-making.

Civic education is forward-looking. It equips citizens—young and old—with the habits, tools, and confidence to protect truth and keep democracy resilient.

What are they trying to make you believe? Keep citizens uninformed, making them vulnerable to misinformation and disengagement.

What's the countermove? Teach civic skills early and often, so citizens grow up with democratic "muscle memory."

Reflection: Educate for Resilience
Where in your life — your school, workplace, or community — could you introduce more civic learning? What simple action could strengthen the shield against misinformation?

A simple 30-Day Civic Sprint Playbook is included in the Appendix to help schools, libraries, or local groups practice these habits.

The Power of Collective Hope

When life feels heavy, it is tempting to believe your actions don't matter. But communities don't survive hard times by luck. They endure because enough people decide not to give up—and because hope becomes stronger when it is shared.

Think of civil rights marchers who linked arms through fear, or neighbors who formed human chains to rescue flood victims. None of those acts began with certainty of success; they began with trust that working together would create possibilities larger than any one individual could achieve.

Shared hope is not about ignoring problems. It is about trusting connection over isolation. Each small act—a teacher creating a dialogue club, a worker rallying colleagues, neighbors pooling resources in a tough economy — says, "You are not alone." That message builds a foundation for resilience stronger than any law or institution.

What ties this chapter together is simple and powerful: resilience grows when people believe in one another enough to keep showing up. Trust multiplies when it is shared, and shared trust is the deepest form of hope.

What are they trying to make you believe? Spread cynicism; convince people that nothing they do will matter.

What's the countermove? Share hope through trust and connection—remind people they are not alone, and that small steps become powerful when multiplied across a community.

Reflection: Extend a Hand Across Difference

Imagine a handshake—literal or symbolic—with someone on "the other side" of an issue in your life. Who might that be? What small gesture could you offer that would rebuild trust and show that shared hope is still possible?

Chapter 8: Democracy for All: Centering Diversity and Global Perspectives

"The best way to predict the future is to create it." — Peter Drucker

The story of democracy is never finished. Every generation inherits its strengths and its struggles and decides whether to protect, repair, or neglect them. Today, the weight of that choice rests with us.

We live in a moment of turbulence: rising polarization, endless disinformation, and global crises that ripple into local lives. But this chapter isn't about despair. It's about what comes next. Democracy is not a relic to be admired or a machine to be maintained; it is a living practice, built every day by people who care enough to shape it.

In these pages, we'll explore the innovations that can make systems more inclusive, the cultural habits that keep communities resilient, and the small but powerful ways individuals can push the future toward fairness, trust, and hope.

The future of democracy will not be written in some distant capital; it's being written right now in classrooms, workplaces, neighborhoods, and online spaces. The question is simple but urgent: what role will you play in writing it?

Innovation at the Edges: Technology as a Democratic Tool

Across the globe, communities are using technology not just to communicate but to reshape how decisions are made. These experiments remind us that democracy doesn't have to be confined to voting every few years—it can be a daily practice of dialogue and decision-making.

In Taiwan, the government created the vTaiwan platform after mass student protests in 2014. Citizens debated online, offered proposals, and helped shape national policy. Instead of being dominated by the loudest voices, the platform used AI-assisted tools to cluster opinions and highlight areas of agreement. The result: decisions that reflected broad consensus, not just partisan division.

Elsewhere, cities from Porto Alegre in Brazil to Paris and New York have pioneered participatory budgeting, letting citizens directly decide how to spend portions of public funds. The process not only gives residents a voice in priorities—parks, schools, and safety — but also builds trust that government responds to genuine needs.

Technology also offers potential tools for inclusion. Translation software helps immigrants take part in public meetings. Digital forums make it easier for busy parents and workers to weigh in. But not every innovation is risk-free. Blockchain voting, sometimes hailed as the future, raises serious security concerns, and poorly moderated online platforms can amplify misinformation as easily as they share truth.

The lesson? Technology is not a cure-all. It is a tool—powerful when combined with transparency, inclusivity, and safeguards, but dangerous when adopted uncritically.

What are they trying to make you believe? Restrict democratic participation to a few voices, leaving decisions in the hands of elites or the most powerful.

What's the countermove? Use technology thoughtfully to widen the circle of participation—while staying vigilant against risks of manipulation or exclusion.

Reflection: Innovation in Your Community
What decision in your town, school, or workplace could benefit from more voices? How might technology help gather ideas, bridge distance, or highlight consensus?

Global Lessons in Diversity and Inclusion

Democracy is not a single formula. It looks different in every country, shaped by culture, history, and the needs of the people who practice it. While technology offers new ways to innovate, some of the most enduring lessons come from communities that expanded democracy by including voices once pushed to the margins.

Brazil: The Birthplace of Participatory Budgeting
In the late 1980s, the Brazilian city of Porto Alegre launched a bold experiment: letting citizens decide directly how to spend portions of the city budget. Thousands of residents gathered in neighborhood assemblies, debated priorities, and voted on projects—schools, sanitation, housing. The model spread across the globe, from Paris to New York, proving that democracy deepens when people can see their voices shaping tangible results.

India: Village Assemblies and Direct Democracy
In rural India, Gram Sabhas (village assemblies) give citizens a direct say in local priorities—water projects, roads, and schools. On paper, they embody the promise of grassroots democracy: decisions made close to the people, in open forums where anyone can speak.

But the reality is more complex. Caste hierarchies, gender barriers, and elite capture often distort participation. In some regions, the most powerful families dominate decision-making, while women and marginalized groups struggle to be heard. Yet even with these challenges, Gram Sabhas remain a vital experiment—proof that democracy is at its strongest when it adapts to local traditions and continually pushes for broader inclusion.

Rwanda: Women at the Center of Governance

After the devastation of the 1990s genocide, Rwanda rebuilt with gender equity as a central pillar. Today, women hold over 60% of parliamentary seats—the highest percentage in the world. This shift has influenced national priorities, from education to healthcare. It shows that democracy grows stronger when diverse voices shape the agenda at the highest levels.

New Zealand: Māori Co-Governance

In New Zealand, Māori communities have secured co-governance arrangements over rivers, forests, and sacred lands. These models blend indigenous traditions with modern democratic systems, ensuring that cultural values and sovereignty are not symbolic add-ons but central to decision-making. Democracy here means honoring multiple traditions in one shared framework.

Finland: Civic Education as a Shield

In Finland, civic education is built into school curricula from an early age. Students don't just memorize facts about government; they learn to spot misinformation, evaluate sources, and debate current issues respectfully. This long-term investment shows how teaching democratic skills early can protect societies against disinformation and polarization.

Together, these examples highlight a powerful truth: democracy thrives when it includes diversity. The more voices at the table—

across class, gender, culture, and history—the more resilient and creative democracy becomes.

What are they trying to make you believe? Assume democracy is one-size-fits-all, limiting imagination to a single model.

What's the countermove? Learn from global practices—borrowing, adapting, and honoring diverse approaches that expand participation and strengthen trust.

Reflection: Learning Across Borders
Which of these global practices—participatory budgeting, village assemblies, gender inclusion, indigenous co-governance, or civic education—feels most relevant to your community? How might you adapt a version to enrich participation where you live?

Learning From Setbacks: How Movements Rebuild

Every democracy faces setbacks. Movements stall, reforms get rolled back, and cynicism creeps in when progress feels out of reach. But history shows that defeats don't just test democracy—they force it to develop.

The U.S. civil rights movement, for example, adapted after early legal defeats by shifting tactics: from courtroom battles to mass direct action, from isolated protests to nationwide coalitions. In South Africa, anti-apartheid organizers pivoted from domestic demonstrations to international boycotts and sanctions when repression grew too harsh. In Eastern Europe, activists turned to underground schools, cultural groups, and secret networks that kept civic identity alive until the moment of change arrived.

These setbacks were painful, but they became catalysts for reinvention. Movements learned to diversify strategies, broaden their alliances, and prepare for the long haul.

Hope matters not because it ignores struggle, but because it makes reinvention possible. Every failure is a lesson, every pause an opportunity to build strength for the next phase.

What are they trying to make you believe? Use setbacks and defeats to convince citizens that change is impossible.

What's the countermove? Treat setbacks as opportunities to innovate—pivoting strategies, expanding alliances, and finding new ways to keep democracy alive.

Reflection: Reinvention After Loss
Think of a time when you or your community faced a major obstacle. How did it change the way you approached the problem? What lessons from that pivot could apply to strengthening democracy today?

The Road Ahead

The road ahead for democracy is neither smooth nor guaranteed. Polarization, disinformation, and authoritarian pressures remain real. But the lessons from around the world show us that democracy doesn't survive by standing still—it survives by adapting.

Innovation matters: from Taiwan's digital platforms to Brazil's participatory budgeting, citizens are reshaping how decisions get made. Diversity matters: Rwanda's women in parliament, New Zealand's co-governance with Māori, and Finland's civic education model prove that broader inclusion makes systems more resilient. Resilience matters: Poland's Solidarity and countless grassroots movements remind us that setbacks can fuel reinvention, not defeat.

The next chapter of democracy won't be written in theory—it will be written by ordinary citizens choosing to act. And here is the key: democracies that embrace diversity and innovation don't just endure—they flourish.

What are they trying to make you believe? Convince people that democracy is too broken to fix, and that their efforts won't matter.

What's the countermove? Refuse despair. Choose innovation, inclusion, and resilience as the building blocks of a democracy that is more inclusive, more responsive, and more alive than before.

Reflection: The Next Step Is Yours
What one action—digital, local, or personal—will you take to strengthen democracy in your sphere of influence? Write it down, share it with someone you trust, and commit to taking that step this week.

.

Chapter 9: Choosing Hope: Renewal, Resilience, and the Future We Build Together

"Hope is not a lottery ticket you can sit on the sofa and clutch, feeling lucky. It is an axe you break down doors with in an emergency." — Rebecca Solnit

Every democracy is tested. Crises strike, leaders fail, disinformation floods our screens, and divisions deepen until it feels like trust itself has collapsed. In moments like these, it is tempting to believe that democracy is fragile by nature—that it cannot withstand the storms of our age.

But history proves otherwise. Again and again, citizens have shown that when institutions wobble, ordinary people step forward. They gather in squares with candles, draft new constitutions from living rooms, form food networks in disasters, and build trust one conversation at a time. Resilience doesn't come from avoiding hardship; it comes from facing it together.

This final chapter is about what happens *after the storm*. It is about the practices that allow democracies not just to survive disruption, but to emerge stronger: crisis response rooted in people power, everyday tools to track progress, digital platforms that can expand participation, and, above all, the decision to act with hope.

The future of democracy won't be decided by experts alone. It will be decided by what citizens choose to do when tested—by the habits they carry, the courage they share, and the actions they take today.

What are they trying to make you believe? Convince citizens that democracy is too weak to survive crises, so they should retreat or stay silent.

What's the countermove? Show that resilience is built in action—when people refuse despair, organize, and adapt, turning crises into opportunities for renewal.

Reflection: Your Role in the Storm
When your community faces its next crisis—whether political, social, or environmental—what role do you imagine yourself playing? What is one step you could prepare to take now?

Appendix C: Civic Action Tools includes a Democracy Tracker you can use to log your own contributions.

Resilience in Crisis: How Democracies Bounce Back (and How You Can Help)

When crises hit, democracies are often declared too slow, too messy, too fragile to cope. Yet history shows the opposite: moments of upheaval can become catalysts for renewal when citizens refuse to retreat and instead step forward together.

South Korea: The Candlelight Revolution
In 2016–2017, millions of South Koreans took to the streets with candles in hand, protesting corruption at the highest levels of government. Night after night, families, students, and workers filled public squares—peacefully, persistently, insistently. Their protests led to the impeachment of President Park Geun-hye and reaffirmed the power of collective action in a modern democracy. What could have become a legitimacy crisis instead became proof of democratic resilience.

Iceland: Rebuilding After Collapse
After the 2008 financial meltdown, Icelanders didn't simply endure the crisis; they demanded structural change. Citizens gathered in public forums, crowdsourced input online, and drafted a new constitutional proposal. Though political leaders later stalled its implementation, the process itself showed how ordinary people could reimagine governance after collapse, planting seeds that continue to influence Icelandic politics.

Local Lessons
Democracy's resilience isn't only written in capitals. After natural disasters, communities often organize faster than governments: neighbors check on one another, set up temporary shelters, and coordinate relief before official help arrives. These everyday crisis responses show the same truth as national movements: democracy bends but doesn't break when citizens take ownership.

The pattern is apparent: crises reveal the weakness of top-down systems that rely on perfect leaders. But they also reveal the strength of bottom-up resilience when people act with persistence, creativity, and solidarity.

What are they trying to make you believe? Use crises to suspend democracy, claiming that emergencies require silencing dissent and concentrating power.

What's the countermove? Treat crises as moments to expand democracy—where citizens organize, deliberate, and hold leaders accountable, proving that resilience grows from the ground up.

Reflection: Crisis as a Turning Point
Think about a crisis you've lived through—local, national, or global. What role did ordinary people play in responding? How could those

same habits of solidarity and creativity prepare your community for the next test?

Cultivating Hope: Why Optimism Is a Civic Responsibility

Hope isn't just an emotion. In a democracy, it's a civic duty. When people believe change is impossible, they stop taking part—leaving the field to those who would rather concentrate power or spread fear. Choosing hope is therefore not a private act of optimism; it's a public contribution to resilience.

Documented Lessons in Civic Hope

- South Africa's Truth and Reconciliation process worked because citizens believed the future was worth building together, even after decades of division. Hope gave them the courage to face pain in the open.

- The U.S. civil rights movement sustained itself on "freedom songs," church gatherings, and marches that infused exhausted activists with energy to keep going. Hope was not naïve—it was fuel for persistence.

- Post-conflict Northern Ireland shows how fragile peace still requires hope. Cross-community programs—schools, sports, and youth exchanges—helped sustain trust long after the Good Friday Agreement, proving that hope must be practiced to endure.

Practical Habits of Civic Hope

- Gratitude Journals with a Civic Lens: Instead of only listing personal positives, note daily moments of democracy working—neighbors helping neighbors, a fair decision at work, a respectful debate online. These reminders ground us in the evidence that progress exists.

- Future-Casting Exercises: Imagine your community five years from now if people choose connection over division. Visualizing a better future makes it easier to act toward it.

- Symbols and Rituals: From candlelight vigils in South Korea to yellow umbrellas in Hong Kong, symbols transform private hope into collective energy.

What are they trying to make you believe? Spread despair, convince citizens nothing will ever change, so they stop taking part.

What's the countermove? Practice civic hope, use gratitude, storytelling, and symbols to sustain collective courage, turning hope into a renewable resource for democracy.

Reflection: Practicing Hope
What symbol, story, or daily practice keeps you connected to the belief that change is possible? How might you share it with others to strengthen hope in your community?

Appendix D: Reflection Prompts collects all the questions from each chapter to help you journal and practice civic hope

Building Your Crisis Action Plan

Resilience isn't built in the moment of crisis—it's built in advance. Just as families prepare emergency kits for storms or earthquakes, democracies grow stronger when citizens prepare civic "resilience kits" for political, social, or environmental shocks.

A Crisis Action Plan doesn't need to be complex. It starts with three simple questions:

1. Who will you check on? List of neighbors, friends, or vulnerable community members who might need help.
2. How will you connect? Identify the group chats, forums, or meeting spots where people can share updates and coordinate quickly.
3. What resources can you share? From blankets to skills to reliable information, resilience grows when everyone contributes what they can.

Start small. Four friends around a kitchen table. A handful of neighbors in the living room. Use a shared document or group chat to track tasks. Set one simple goal: deliver supplies, gather signatures, clean up a block and celebrate the win. Small victories build confidence for larger ones.

This isn't just disaster preparedness. It's democracy in action: citizens choosing to organize instead of waiting for someone else to fix the problem.

What are they trying to make you believe? Convince people that crises must be handled only by professionals or governments, leaving ordinary citizens sidelined.

What's the countermove? Build crisis action plans in advance—empowering communities to act quickly, support one another, and prove that resilience is strongest when it's shared.

Reflection: Your Crisis Readiness
If a major disruption hit your community tomorrow, what role would you want to play? Who would you check on, and how would you stay connected? Write down one concrete step you can take this month to put your plan into practice.

Measuring Your Impact: Tracking Progress in Everyday Democracy

Democracy can feel thankless when small actions disappear into the noise. A single petition signed, or a single meeting attended might feel like a drop in the ocean. But drops add up to tides, and resilient communities know how to track their momentum.

A **democracy tracker** can be as simple as a notebook or spreadsheet. Write each step: attending a council meeting, correcting misinformation, mentoring a first-time voter. Over time, the pattern becomes clear—you are building civic muscle. What once felt invisible becomes visible.

Communities are already experimenting with shared dashboards. In some towns, volunteers log hours or signatures collected, creating live portraits of civic energy. Schools post "impact maps" with pins marking every cleanup, petition, or public comment. These visuals inspire newcomers and reassure veterans alike, the work matters.

Digital tools expand the possibilities. Apps let volunteers coordinate, share updates, and celebrate milestones. But low-tech rituals matter too: a potluck where each person shares one civic win, or a bulletin board for weekly shoutouts. Recognition prevents burnout and reinforces the truth: Democracy grows where encouragement takes root.

Tracking isn't bureaucracy; it's fuel. It reminds us that resilience isn't built in sudden bursts, but in steady steps multiplied across many people.

What are they trying to make you believe? Convince citizens their efforts are too small to matter, draining energy through invisibility and discouragement.

What's the countermove? Make impact visible. Track progress—personal or collective—so every action builds confidence, sustains energy, and inspires the next step.

Reflection: Your Democracy Tracker
What's one way you could record your own civic contributions, big or small? A journal? A shared spreadsheet? A whiteboard on the fridge? Choose one method and try logging your wins for a week. Notice how it changes your sense of impact.

Building Digital Democracy: Tools for the Next Generation

If democracy once seemed locked in marble halls, technology has pried open the doors. Today, people can take part not only by casting a ballot every few years but by shaping daily decisions through digital tools.

Practical Innovations
- Participatory budgeting apps let citizens vote directly on spending priorities—a skatepark, bike lanes, or public Wi-Fi.
- Verified online petitions now carry weight, allowing local and national governments to gauge citizen priorities more effectively.
- Hackathons and civic tech projects produce apps that translate policies into plain language, remind citizens of voting deadlines, or make complex laws easier to navigate.

Case in Point: Taiwan's vTaiwan Project
In Taiwan, the vTaiwan platform invited citizens into debates on issues from Uber regulation to pandemic response. Instead of online

shouting matches, the platform used AI-assisted tools to highlight areas of consensus.

Policymakers then integrated this feedback directly into lawmaking. The result: digital democracy that translated public input into real policy impact.

Why It Matters
These tools widen participation. Busy parents can weigh in from their phones. Immigrants can contribute through translation software. Young people—digital natives—can step into civic life where they already live: online.

But technology is no magic wand. Without privacy safeguards, transparency, and inclusive design, digital tools risk amplifying the loudest voices or reinforcing inequities. True digital democracy must serve the many, not just the tech-savvy few.

What are they trying to make you believe? Keep decision-making locked in elite spaces, using complexity and distance to discourage ordinary participation.

What's the countermove? Use digital tools—designed for accessibility, transparency, and inclusion—to break barriers, invite more voices, and ensure public input translates into real outcomes.

Reflection: Your Digital Step
What digital tool could you use—or even help create—to expand participation in your community? Imagine a simple platform for your school, neighborhood, or workplace. How could it turn ideas into action?

Figure 12: A citizen engages in digital democracy — symbolizing the growing role of technology in expanding participation and shaping civic life (Author-Created).

Beyond the Bubble: Digital Platforms for Democracy

The internet is often blamed for fueling echo chambers—spaces where people only hear voices that reinforce what they already believe. And it's true: poorly designed platforms can harden polarization and spread misinformation at lightning speed. But the same technology can also widen perspectives when built for transparency, inclusion, and genuine dialogue.

Brazil: Porto Alegre's Participatory Platforms
In Porto Alegre, Brazil—the birthplace of participatory budgeting—digital platforms expanded local assemblies into online spaces. Residents proposed projects, debated priorities, and voted on everything from sanitation improvements to public transportation. What once required in-person meetings in crowded halls became more accessible to parents, workers, and young people who could now log in and contribute.

Spain: Decide Madrid
In Madrid, the city created *Decide Madrid*, a digital platform where citizens could propose and vote on policies. Some proposals became binding city law, showing that digital forums weren't just symbolic—they carried genuine power. By opening the debate to thousands of

residents, the platform gave legitimacy to voices often excluded from traditional politics.

Why It Matters These examples show online spaces don't have to be breeding grounds for division. With the right design principles—open access, strong moderation, verified participation—they can create bridges across difference. Digital platforms can transform disagreement from a shouting match into a structured dialogue where common ground becomes visible.

What are they trying to make you believe? Trap citizens in echo chambers, using algorithms and polarization to weaken trust and shut down dialogue.

What's the countermove? Build and use platforms that widen participation, verify voices, and deliberately create space for respectful debate—turning the internet into a tool for democracy rather than division.

Reflection: Escaping the Bubble
Think about the digital spaces you spend the most time in. Do they expose you to different perspectives, or only reinforce what you already believe? What small step could you take—joining a new forum, hosting a cross-perspective discussion, or supporting an inclusive platform—to help burst your own bubble?

Your Democracy Journey: The Challenge to Take Action Today

As you close this book, take stock of the journey you've traveled. Together we have explored resilience in communities, learned from global movements, and seen how hope—when shared—becomes a civic responsibility. We've examined the tools that widen participation and the daily habits that keep democracy alive.

The lesson is clear: democracy is not a gift handed down fully formed. It is built and rebuilt in every generation. It is fragile, yes, but also renewable—because it depends on the choices of ordinary people like you.

Your task is not to carry the weight of the entire system alone. It is to take one step, then another, and to join your voice with others. Small actions when tracked, shared, and multiplied create momentum. Local victories ripple outward. Courage spreads. Hope expands.

Your Three Anchors

- **Resilience**: You have seen how communities withstand storms and crises when they act together.
- **Diversity and Innovation:** You have learned how global voices and creative tools expand what democracy can look like.
- **Hope in Action:** You have discovered that hope is not passive—it is the energy that sustains persistence and progress.

The future of democracy will not be written in distant capitals or by experts alone. It will be written in living rooms, classrooms, workplaces, and digital platforms—anywhere people decide to act with courage and connection.

What are they trying to make you believe? Convince you that democracy is too broken, too distant, too complicated to be worth your effort.

What's the countermove? Remember the journey you've just taken.

Act—however small—knowing that resilience grows with each step, diversity strengthens every system, and hope multiplies when shared.

Reflection: Write Your Next Chapter
What one action will you take this week to carry forward resilience, innovation, and hope? Write it down, commit to it, and share it with someone who will hold you accountable. Then, take the step. The story of democracy is still being written—let your chapter be one of renewal.

Figure 13: A vote cast into the ballot box — symbolizing how every action, big or small, can shape the future (Author-Created).

Conclusion

"Democracy is never a final achievement. It is a call to an untiring effort." — John F. Kennedy

If you've made it to this last page, pause for a moment. Look around you—maybe you're riding a bus, or sitting at your kitchen table, or tucked away in the back corner of a library. Wherever you are, know this: you are part of the living story of democracy. You may not feel it every day, but your voice, your choices, and your presence matter more than you think.

Perhaps you opened this book feeling tired, cynical, or even powerless—searching for clarity in a world that feels endlessly divided. I understand that feeling; I've felt it too. In writing these pages, I had to remind myself again and again that democracy isn't about perfect plans or flawless leaders. It's about ordinary people—people like you and me—deciding to care enough to keep showing up. Sometimes in bold, visible ways, but more often in quiet, steady actions that rarely make headlines yet hold everything together.

Democracy isn't a machine you switch on every four years, or a building you can abandon once constructed. It is a living practice: fragile, frustrating, unfinished. It is built and rebuilt, generation after generation, by those who refuse to give up on one another. That is the heartbeat I hope you've heard pulsing through these chapters: democracy isn't "out there," distant and untouchable. It is right here, wherever you are, waiting for you to take part.

Think of the road we've traveled together. We began in the fog of confusion, where misinformation and division make it easy to wonder if anything matters. The traps of doomscrolling and the ways digital platforms box us in were examined. We looked at the cracks in our systems—and the unexpected places where repair begins. Along the way, we heard stories of resilience from towns and cities across the world: people who could have walked away, but stepped forward.

You now hold a toolkit in your hands. Fact-checking, building bridges, and starting small: you know how to do these things. You've seen that democracy isn't only for the loudest voices or the most confident experts—it belongs to anyone willing to practice, to stumble, to learn, and to keep going. You don't need to save the world alone. With care and courage, you just need to tend your corner of it.

Here's the truth I want to leave you with: hope is not soft. It is not a dream. Hope is disciplined. The subject is stubborn. The act is choosing to plant seeds when storms are overhead. It's checking a rumor before sharing it, listening to a neighbor's story, helping someone cast their first ballot, or speaking up when silence would be easier. It is showing up, even when you feel unsure. These are minor acts, but repeated across millions of lives, they become the foundation of trust and the spark of renewal.

And if you feel too small, too tired, or too ordinary, remember this: every grand movement in history began with people who had every reason to doubt themselves, yet refused to quit. Every lasting change was seeded by small groups who acted, anyway. Your voice may feel like a whisper, but when joined with others, it becomes a chorus.

So, I leave you with one challenge: choose one concrete step, this week, that makes democracy more real in your life. Start a conversation with someone who disagrees with you. Sign up for a local meeting. Mentor a new voter. Share an accurate story instead of a rumor. Write it down. Tell a friend. Make it real. Small steps multiplied create culture.

And don't do it alone. Join our companion community if you need support. Share your "democracy wins." Learn from others. Celebrate the brief victories. Together we create momentum that no setback can erase.

Thank you for staying with me through these pages—for wrestling with doubt, for daring to believe your participation matters. By reading, reflecting, and acting, you are now part of something far larger: the global, ongoing movement of ordinary people keeping democracy alive.

In the end, democracy's promise is not secured by speeches or laws alone. It is kept alive by neighbors who look out for one another, by students who ask inconvenient questions, by workers who refuse silence, and by communities that keep showing up. That's where the authentic story of democracy is written.

So take your next step. Add your line to the story. The book of democracy is not finished—it is being written by you, right now, in the choices you make and the courage you show. And that, more than anything, gives me hope.

And if you're wondering where to begin, turn to the appendix. The checklists there are simple tools you can use right now to evaluate leaders and reflect on your own role as a citizen. They're a starting point — small steps that can guide you as you take your place in the unfinished story of democracy.

Acknowledgments

This book would not have come to life without the encouragement and support of the people surrounding me.

To my dear friends, who listened patiently, asked thoughtful questions, and reminded me why truth and democracy matter — your voices helped shape these pages.

A special thank you to the Tuesday Coffee Club not only for the laughter and conversations that fueled my spirit but also for reading an early draft and giving me honest, thoughtful feedback. Your insights helped polish this work and gave me the confidence to share it with the world.

To my Mastermind group, your encouragement, wisdom, and accountability pushed me forward when doubts crept in. Thank you for reminding me that big goals are reached step by step, with persistence and heart.

And to everyone who believes in the quiet power of ordinary citizens — this book is for you. Together, we are the guardians of truth and freedom.

References

Note: Some links in this References section may not appear as live hyperlinks in all e-readers. If so, simply copy and paste the full URL into your web browser.

1. American Philosophical Association. (2022, March 23). Doomscrolling and the unspeakable. Retrieved from https://blog.apaonline.org/2022/03/23/doomscrolling-and-the-unspeakable/
2. American Sociological Association. (n.d.). Black Lives Matter: Lessons from a global movement. Retrieved from https://www.theasa.net/black-lives-matter-lessons-global-movement
3. Arao, B., & Clemens, K. (2013). From safe spaces to brave spaces. Retrieved from https://www.anselm.edu/sites/default/files/Documents/Center%20for%20Teaching%20Excellence/From%20Safe%20Spaces%20to%20Brave%20Spaces.pdf
4. Arizona State University. (2021). The science of hope: More than wishful thinking. Retrieved from https://news.asu.edu/20210615-solutions-science-hope-more-wishful-thinking
5. Bajpai, N., & Sachs, J. (2011). Strengthening Gram Sabhas: Village democracy in India. Columbia University. Retrieved from https://academiccommons.columbia.edu/doi/10.7916/D8DV1QS8
6. Bhojwani, S. (2016). Immigrant voices make democracy stronger. ESL Bits. Retrieved from https://esl-bits.eu/advanced.listening/Media/2016-10-28/Sayu.Bhojwani/default.html
7. Bouckaert, L. (n.d.). About deep democracy. Retrieved from https://bouckaert.nu/en/about-deep-democracy/
8. Braver Angels. (n.d.). Building a house united. Retrieved [insert date of access], from https://braverangels.org/

9. Brennan Center for Justice. (2020). How to fact-check the Trump-Biden debates. Retrieved from https://www.brennancenter.org/our-work/analysis-opinion/how-fact-check-trump-biden-debates
10. Brennan Center for Justice. (2023). How to detect and guard against deceptive AI-generated election information. Retrieved from https://www.brennancenter.org/our-work/research-reports/how-detect-and-guard-against-deceptive-ai-generated-election-information
11. Britell, R. (2018). Lessons from America's greatest grassroots campaigns. Retrieved from https://www.britell.com/lessons-from-americas-great-grassroots-campaigns/
12. Brookings Institution. (2018). The bucket list for involved citizens: 76 things you can do to boost civic engagement. Retrieved from https://www.brookings.edu/articles/the-bucket-list-for-involved-citizens-76-things-you-can-do-to-boost-civic-engagement/
13. Brookings Institution. (2021). The need for civic education in 21st-century schools. Retrieved from https://www.brookings.edu/articles/the-need-for-civic-education-in-21st-century-schools/
14. Centre for European Policy Studies. (2021). Realising the democratic ideal: Empowering marginalised voices in deliberative democracy. Retrieved from https://www.ceps.eu/ceps-publications/realising-the-democratic-ideal-empowering-marginalised-voices-in-deliberative-democracy/
15. Charpleix, L. (2018). The Whanganui River as Te Awa Tupua: Place-based law in a legally pluralistic society. The Geographical Journal, 184(1), 19–30. https://doi.org/10.1111/geoj.12238
16. Chou, H., & Lee, C. (2024). Social drivers and algorithmic mechanisms on digital media. Frontiers in Psychology, 15, 11373151. https://pmc.ncbi.nlm.nih.gov/articles/PMC11373151/
17. European Partnership for Democracy. (2022). Exploring worldwide democratic innovations: A series of case studies. Retrieved from https://epd.eu/news-publications/exploring-worldwide-democratic-innovations-a-series-of-case-studies/

18. European Partnership for Democracy. (2023). A case study of Taiwan. Retrieved from https://epd.eu/content/uploads/2023/07/Case-Study-Taiwan.pdf
19. Foster-Fishman, P. G., & Keys, C. B. (2011). Measuring the impact of civic engagement. Retrieved from https://www.issuelab.org/resources/12389/12389.pdf
20. Geeks for Geeks. (2021). Pillars of democracy: History, importance, and relation. Retrieved from https://www.geeksforgeeks.org/upsc/pillars-of-democracy/
21. Google News Initiative. (n.d.). Google fact check tools. Retrieved from https://newsinitiative.withgoogle.com/resources/trainings/google-fact-check-tools/
22. Levitsky, S., & Way, L. A. (2010). How Viktor Orbán wins. Journal of Democracy, 21(2), 38–55. https://www.journalofdemocracy.org/articles/how-viktor-orban-wins/
23. Living Room Conversations. (n.d.). What is a living room conversation? Retrieved [insert date of access], from https://livingroomconversations.org/whatislrc/
24. Mashable. (2023). 8 of the loudest calls to action from youth activists in 2023. Retrieved from https://mashable.com/article/youth-activism-2023-so-far
25. Northwestern University Kellogg School of Management. (2020). Take 5: How to talk politics (constructively). Retrieved from https://insight.kellogg.northwestern.edu/article/take-5-how-to-talk-politics-constructively
26. Participedia. (2020). vTaiwan. Retrieved from https://participedia.net/method/vtaiwan
27. Powley, E. (2005). Rwanda: Women hold up half the parliament. International IDEA. Retrieved from https://www.idea.int/news-media/news/rwanda-women-hold-half-parliament

28. Protect Democracy. (2022). The Faithful Fight toolkit: Building bridges across difference. Retrieved from https://protectdemocracy.org/work/building-bridges-across-difference/

29. Pew Research Center. (2019). Trust and distrust in America. Retrieved from https://www.pewresearch.org/politics/2019/07/22/trust-and-distrust-in-america/

30. Sage Journals. (2024). Democratic resilience in the twenty-first century. Political Studies, 72(3), 457–479. https://doi.org/10.1177/00323217251345779

31. Scientific American. (2023). Political attacks on libraries endanger small-town democracy. Retrieved from https://www.scientificamerican.com/article/political-attacks-on-libraries-endanger-small-town-democracy/

32. SHS Conferences. (2024). Echo chambers and algorithmic bias. SHS Web of Conferences, icense2024, 05001. https://www.shs-conferences.org/articles/shsconf/pdf/2024/22/shsconf_icense2024_05001.pdf

33. Staffbase. (2020). The ultimate guide to engaging virtual town halls. Retrieved from https://staffbase.com/blog/the-ultimate-guide-to-virtual-town-halls

34. Tufts University, Center for Information and Research on Civic Learning and Engagement (CIRCLE). (2024). Young people and the 2024 election. Retrieved from https://circle.tufts.edu/latest-research/2024-poll-barriers-issues-economy

35. Tutu, D. (1999). No future without forgiveness. Doubleday. https://www.goodreads.com/book/show/78038.No_Future_Without_Forgiveness

36. Twain, M. (n.d.). Quote about patriotism. Retrieved from https://www.brainyquote.com/quotes/mark_twain_101452

37. UNICEF. (2023). A quick guide to spotting misinformation. Retrieved from https://www.unicef.org/eca/stories/quick-guide-spotting-misinformation

38. U.S. Election Assistance Commission. (n.d.). Language access resources. Retrieved from https://www.eac.gov/language-access-resources

39. University of Cambridge. (2019). Faith in democracy: Millennials are the most disillusioned. Retrieved from https://www.cam.ac.uk/stories/youthanddemocracy

40. University of Iowa. (n.d.). Active listening | Conflict management. Retrieved from https://conflictmanagement.org.uiowa.edu/active-listening

41. VolunteerMatch. (n.d.). Where volunteering begins. Retrieved from https://www.volunteermatch.org/

42. Wikipedia. (n.d.). Democratic backsliding. Retrieved from https://en.wikipedia.org/wiki/Democratic_backsliding

43. World Economic Forum. (2020). Why Finland is leading the fight against fake news. Retrieved from https://www.weforum.org/agenda/2020/03/finland-fake-news-education/

Leave Review

A Personal Request

Thank you for reading *A Reminder of What Democracy Is*.
When I started writing this book, I realized that many people — myself included, were feeling helpless and uncertain about how to make a difference. We care deeply about our country, yet it's easy to feel as if our individual voices no longer matter.

Through the conversations I've had, I've learned that this feeling is shared by so many. What I've also discovered is that confidence and understanding can grow again when we see how democracy truly works and how much power we each hold when we show up, speak up, and take part.

If this book gave you clarity, encouragement, or even one small idea you can carry forward, I would be deeply grateful if you took a few minutes to leave a review.

Your review helps others who feel the same uncertainty find this book. It tells them they're not alone, and that change begins with awareness, courage, and connection.

Your voice matters in a democracy, and it matters here, too. Thank you for supporting this work and being part of the conversation. Together, we keep democracy alive.

 Scan the QR code below or visit:
https://tinyurl.com/DemoReview123
(Your honest words help others discover this book and continue the conversation about what democracy truly means.)

Appendix: Tools, Checklists, and Prompts

This appendix is a companion to the book—a set of tools, checklists, and prompts you can return to whenever you want to refresh your role as a citizen, a voter, or simply someone who cares about democracy. Think of it as a practical toolkit to carry forward.

Appendix A: Democracy Job Requirements Checklist

When evaluating candidates for leadership, use this checklist to guide your decision.

☐ **Accountability**—Accepts responsibility and welcomes oversight.

☐ **Transparency**—Communicates clearly and openly about decisions.

☐ **Respect for Law**—Upholds constitutional principles and the rule of law.

☐ **Inclusiveness**—Seeks to represent all citizens, not just one group.

☐ **Integrity**—Acts ethically, even when not being watched.

☐ **Competence**—Demonstrates knowledge and ability to address issues effectively.

☐ **Service**—Places the needs of the community above personal gain.

Ask yourself: Does this candidate consistently demonstrate these qualities?

Appendix B: Responsibilities of a Democratic Voter

Democracy thrives when citizens take their roles seriously. Use this checklist to reflect on your participation.

☐ **Stay Informed**—Seek reliable sources and question misinformation.

☐ **Engage Respectfully**—Discuss issues across differences with curiosity, not hostility.

☐ **Vote Consistently**—Participate in every election, local and national.

☐ **Hold Leaders Accountable**—Monitor promises and actions after the election.

☐ **Support Fairness**—Defend the rights of others, even those you disagree with.

☐ **Contribute Locally**—Join community meetings, volunteer, or support civic initiatives.

☐ **Ask yourself:** Am I living up to these responsibilities in my daily and civic life?

Appendix C: Civic Action Tools

Democracy Tracker (4-Week Chart)
- Use this chart to log weekly democratic actions. Notice the patterns that form and reflect on your growth.

Action	Week 1	Week 2	Week 3	Week 4
Attend a local meeting	☐	☐	☐	☐
Correct misinformation	☐	☐	☐	☐
Share voter info link	☐	☐	☐	☐
Volunteer 1 hour	☐	☐	☐	☐
Talk across differences	☐	☐	☐	☐
Support local journalism	☐	☐	☐	☐

Democracy Tracker—four-week habit chart (Author-created)

- *Quick-start ideas to track:* share a verified link; attend a meeting; help register a voter; correct misinformation; thank a public servant.

Five-Minute Democracy Bingo
- A playful way to make small civic actions part of daily life. Complete rows or columns and challenge friends to do the same.

Voter link	Fix misinfo	Sign petition	Post volunteer	Remind friend
Thank worker	Share article	Attend meeting	Register 2 voters	Comment live
DM organizer	Read/Podcast	FREE SPACE	Encourage talk	Join forum
1 hr volunteer	Translate info	Fact-check	Support news	Back cause
Talk differences	Help neighbor	Post reminder	Share resource	Support local

Five-Minute Democracy Bingo (Author-created)
- *Sample squares:* share a voter link; fix one misinfo post; sign a petition; post about volunteering; remind a friend about a deadline; thank a poll worker; forward a reputable article; help two friends register; comment on a livestream Q&A; DM an organizer "thanks."

Appendix D: Reflection Prompts

All reflection questions from each chapter in one place. Use them for journaling, group discussions, or quick reminders of how democracy shows up in daily life.

Chapter 1: Why We're Confused and Why It Matters
- When was the last time you felt overwhelmed by political news? What emotions came up?
- How do you currently decide which voices or sources to trust?
- What small shift could you make to bring more clarity into how you engage with news and information?

Chapter 2: Demystifying Democracy: Foundations for Everyone
- How would you explain democracy to someone younger than you (a child, a student, or a friend new to voting)?
- Which part of democracy feels most distant or unclear to you? Why?
- If you could change one rule or structure in how government works, what would it be?

Chapter 3: Threats in the Now: Spotting the Real Problems (and What's Just Noise)

- Think back to the last time you read a "shocking" headline. How did you react?
- What helps you tell the difference between an immediate threat to democracy and a distraction?
- How could you pause before reacting, so you don't get swept up in the noise?

Chapter 4: The Fog of Misinformation
- When was the last time you shared something online you later questioned? What did you learn from that?
- How do you currently fact-check information before passing it on?
- What one habit could you build to resist the pull of misinformation?

Chapter 5: The Hidden Cracks in Democracy
- What "small cracks" do you see in your community that worry you most (e.g., apathy, corruption, division)?
- How can small acts of accountability strengthen those weak spots?
- Who in your local community models integrity and resilience—and what can you learn from them?

Chapter 6: Everyday Actions: Your Personal Democracy Toolkit
- What role fits you best: organizer, supporter, communicator, or connector?
- How many "micro-actions" could you realistically build into your daily routine?
- What would your first civic action plan look like if you wrote it today?

Chapter 7: Building Resilient Communities
- Where do you already see resilience in your community?
- When have you witnessed people coming together in hard times, and how did it shape your perspective?
- What one minor act could you try this month to strengthen your community's web of trust?

- Extra Step: Imagine extending a handshake—literally or symbolically—to someone on the "other side" of a disagreement. Who might that be, and how could that gesture of connection build trust?

Chapter 8: Imagining the Future of Democracy
- What civic innovation excites you most (digital platforms, participatory budgeting, cultural movements)?
- Where do you find your own resilience when setbacks happen?
- If you imagine democracy 20 years from now, what role do you see yourself playing in shaping it?

Chapter 9: Hope and Renewal
- What warning signs worry you most about democracy's health right now?
- Who are the three people you could call if your community faced a crisis?
- What is one hopeful practice (gratitude journaling, future-casting, small wins) you could adopt starting this week?
- What single step will you take this week to move from reflection to action?

Appendix E: 30-Day Civic Sprint Playbook

Why this exists: Big wins start with small, focused bursts of action. This 30-day sprint turns "someone should do something" into "we did"—with 10-minute daily moves, tiny roles, and a clear finish line.

Step 1 — Pick a micro-goal (today)

Choose one concrete, local outcome you can plausibly move in 30 days.
Examples
- Get interpretation added to the next month's city meeting.
- Add a high-visibility crosswalk sign at one intersection.
- Restore the two evening hours at the branch library for a 60-day pilot.

- Recruit 25 first-time attendees to a school board meeting.

Write it with P.E.A.R. (Problem, Evidence, Affected, Request)
Problem: [one sentence]
Evidence: [one stat/quote/photo]
Affected: [who, briefly]
Request: [specific action + date]

Step 2 — Week-by-week plan (10 minutes a day)

Week 1 — Listen & Map (Days 1–7)
Goal: Understand the problem and find your first 5 allies.
Day 1: Draft your P.E.A.R. statement.
Day 2: Find the relevant **Agenda/Minutes** on your city/school website.
Day 3: Pulse check—text 5 neighbors: "Quick Q: have you had trouble with [issue]? 1–2 lines is plenty."
Day 4: Collect **one stat** (20-min spot count, quick search, or 3 quotes).
Day 5: Mini **power map**: Decider / Influencer / Champion / Gatekeeper.
Day 6: Send a 150-word **process email** to the clerk/staff (ask rules/timing, don't advocate yet).
Day 7: Assemble a 1-page **brief** (Problem, Evidence, Affected, Request, contact).
Deliverable: Crisp brief + list of 5 interested people.

Week 2 — Gather & Invite (Days 8–14)
Goal: Move from "me" to "we."
Day 8: Schedule a 45-minute Zoom or library-room huddle.
Day 9: Create a simple **interest form** (name/email/language/how to help).
Day 10: Send 10 personal invites (DM/text/email): "30-day push to [request]. 45-min planning chat [day/time]. Join?"

Day 11: Make a two-image post (stat + human impact).
Day 12: Ask 2 community connectors (PTA lead, librarian, coach) to boost.
Day 13: Draft **agenda**: problem (2m), ask (2m), roles (5m), next steps (5m).
Day 14: Send reminder; note accessibility (captions, interpretation, childcare).
Deliverable: 6–12 RSVPs; roles pre-framed.

Week 3 — Act in Public (Days 15–21)
Goal: Visible action that builds pressure and trust.
Day 15: Run the huddle. Assign micro-roles:
Tracker (updates dashboard) • **Storycatcher** (quotes/photos) • **Process Buddy** (emails clerk/staff) • **Speaker** (60-sec comment) • **Translator** (top 1–2 languages) • **Bridge** (invites skeptics).
Day 16: File **public email comment** (150 words); share deadline with allies.
Day 17: Launch a **24-hr story drive** (1–2 line impacts + optional photo).
Day 18: Deliver your one-page **brief** to decision-makers (+ 1 photo + 3 quotes).
Day 19: Post a **progress update**: where we are → what we heard → our ask.
Day 20: Confirm who will give **60-sec** (and **30-sec backup**) podium comments.
Day 21: Friendly staff check-in: *"Anything we can clarify?"*
Deliverable: Comments filed; human story visible; acknowledgment from staff/board.

Week 4 — Close the Loop (Days 22–30)
Goal: A decision, a pilot, or a calendared next step—with gratitude.
Day 22: Meeting day: speak, log commitments, grab one photo (if allowed).

Day 23: Send **thank-you + recap** to clerk/board (what we heard + next ask).
Day 24: If **yes**: confirm timeline & point person. If "not yet": propose a **60-day pilot**.
Day 25: Publish a **one-screen summary**: Problem → What we did → What changed → What's next.
Day 26: Recruit 2 new helpers with **micro-asks** (translate a paragraph, 15-min count).
Day 27: Log **Outputs** (# comments, attendees), **Outcomes** (decision/progress), **Equity** (who benefited).
Day 28: Send a gentle **nudge** one week before the due date.
Day 29: 20-min reflection with the team (keep/stop/try).
Day 30: Celebrate publicly; credit widely (especially quiet contributors).
Deliverable: Concrete movement (yes, pilot, or next step) + lessons documented.

Step 3 — Pick your sprint path

1. Online-first (asynchronous): Group chat + shared doc + 45-min call.
   Great for translation access, agenda transparency, posting materials.
2. Place-based (hands-on): Quick site counts, library table, photo storyboard.
   Great for crosswalks, hours, signage, maintenance.
3. Phone-friendly (low-screen): Phone tree, printed handout, voicemail script.
   Great for seniors' issues and neighbor-to-neighbor outreach.

10-line Announcement
We're organizing a 30-day push to improve **[specific thing]** at **[location]**.
Why: [1-line impact].
Ask: [specific action + date].

Help (pick one): share a 1–2 line story • join a 45-min planning call • give a 60-sec comment.

Access: [captions/interpretation/child-watch, if applicable].

Sign-up: [short link or QR]. (Nonpartisan, neighbor-led.)

60-second Comment

Good evening. I'm **[Name]** from **[neighborhood]**.

Problem: [1 line]. **Evidence:** [one stat/quote].

Affected: [group]. **Request:** Please **[action]** by **[date]** and report back at the next meeting.

I've submitted **[brief/photos/letters]** and spoken with **[staff name]**. Thank you for your service.

"Bridge" Invite (to a skeptic)

We may see this differently. Would you review our one-page brief and tell us what we're missing?

If you're open, we'd value your perspective on how this could work better for everyone.

Inclusion & Access Checklist
- Translate the 1-pager into the top 1–2 local languages.
- Enable captions; request/offer interpretation.
- Offer a non-social-media info path (library flyer, printed handout).
- Give 5-minute and 50-minute ways to help.
- Center those most affected—invite them to speak first and share credit.

Simple metrics (tie to your Democracy Tracker)
- Participation: # stories collected, # first-time attendees, # comments submitted.
- Equity: Were materials accessible (language, captions, physical access)? Who was represented?
- Movement: Decision made? Pilot approved? Timeline named? Point person assigned?

Log weekly—seeing momentum prevents the "nothing's changing" spiral.

Choose your lane
- Introvert-friendly: Draft the brief, run the tracker, do the spot count, send thank-yous.
- Super busy: One thing/week (agenda check • invite • comment • recap).
- First-timer: Shadow the Speaker/Process Buddy this sprint; lead a micro-task next sprint.

Common speed bumps (and fixes)
- Silence from decision-makers: Thank them + propose a concrete next step (e.g., a 60-day pilot starting [date]).
- Stalled group chat: Post a binary poll: (A) collect 10 quotes or (B) submit comments by Friday?
- Online pushback: Don't spar; return to process: "Here's the agenda item and our 1-pager. We'll share the outcome."

Keep it healthy
- Two-hour rule: If a task takes >2 hours solo, split it into two 30-min tasks and delegate the rest.
- Rotate roles each sprint; cross-train to prevent burnout.
- Close meetings with one sentence of appreciation.

Appendix F: Vigilance in Action

Authoritarian backsliding rarely happens overnight. It arrives in small steps — procedural tweaks, rule changes, and "emergencies" that never quite end. The best defense is not panic, but vigilance: noticing patterns, keeping records, and speaking up before small changes add up.

Use this checklist to guide your vigilance:

☐ **Track patterns, not just incidents.** Keep a simple log of policy changes, public statements, or procedural shifts. Write down the date, source, and impact.

☐ **Callout normalization.** When something unacceptable is framed as "business as usual," point it out publicly — in conversations, at community meetings, or online.

☐ **Support independent journalism.** Subscribe, donate, or share credible reporting that holds power accountable. Independent media is a frontline defense.

☐ **Back judicial oversight.** Pay attention to local and national courts. Support reforms and watchdog groups that protect judicial independence.

☐ **Vote in every election.** Institutional shifts often start locally. School boards, city councils, and county offices shape the rules that ripple upward.

☐ **Document and share.** When you see concerning patterns, compile your evidence and share with civic organizations, watchdog groups, or local journalists.

☐ **Stay connected.** Build networks with neighbors, coworkers, and community leaders who can respond collectively if rights or processes are threatened.

Reflection: Practicing Vigilance

What's one pattern you've noticed in your community, workplace, or online that worries you?

How could you track it with a quick note on your phone, a folder of clippings, or a simple spreadsheet?

Who could you share your observations with so you're not carrying the weight alone?

Write down one step you'll take this month to practice vigilance in action.

Appendix G: Digital Defense Checklist

There isn't a single app that can "truth-proof" your feed. Tools change. Principles last. Use this checklist to strengthen your everyday digital literacy across any platform:

☐ **Read laterally**. Open a new tab and see how multiple credible outlets cover the same claim. Look for bylines, sourcing, and corroboration.

☐ **Trace the source**. Follow quotes, screenshots, and stats back to the original document, full video, or primary reporting.

☐ **Check timing and context**. Verify dates, locations, and whether old footage is being presented as new. Be cautious with dramatic "breaking" posts that lack details.

☐ **Verify visuals**. Use reverse image or reverse video searches. Look for reuse of the same image elsewhere or inconsistencies (lighting, reflections, lip sync).

☐ **Compare coverage**. Check local reporting, specialist outlets, and a range of credible perspectives. True and important stories will gain independent confirmation.

☐ **Mind the emotions**. Outrage and triumph are attention magnets. When a post spikes your feelings, pause and recheck before you share.

☐ **Step outside the feed**. For research, use private/incognito windows or a separate browser profile to reduce personalization. Balance feeds with newsletters, podcasts, or print.

☐ **Use the "two-person rule."** Before amplifying a hot claim, ask one trusted friend to sanity-check it. Community verification beats speed.

☐ **Share corrections with care**. If you spread something wrong, post a clear update with a source. Model the behavior you want in your circles.

Note: Fact-checking sites and browser "trust" signals can help, but they're not infallible. Treat them as inputs to your judgment, not substitutes for it.

Reflection: Practicing Digital Defense
Think about your own habits online:

1. Which of these checks do you already use?
2. Which one could you add this week to strengthen your digital defenses?
3. Who in your circle could you invite to practice these habits with you?
4. Write one specific change you'll make this month to become a steadier digital defender.

Remember: vigilance is not about fear. It's about steady attention and collective action. Democracies weaken when people shrug off the "small stuff." They grow stronger when citizens track, question, and respond — together.

☐ **Spot the clickbait**. Watch for headlines designed to shock, scare, or outrage you into clicking. Ask: Is this informing me — or provoking me? Check if the article actually matches the headline.

www.ingramcontent.com/pod-product-compliance
Lightning Source LLC
Chambersburg PA
CBHW020547030426
42337CB00013B/1000